Needle-Felted Character Dolls

Needle-Felted Character Dolls

Step-by-step instructions for Fairy,
Mermaid, Rabbit, and more

Mihoko Ueno

STACKPOLE BOOKS

Guilford, Connecticut

Published by Stackpole Books
An imprint of The Rowman & Littlefield Publishing Group, Inc.
4501 Forbes Blvd., Ste. 200
Lanham, MD 20706
www.rowman.com

Distributed by NATIONAL BOOK NETWORK
800-462-6420

Copyright ©2012 Mihoko Ueno
YOUMOU DE TSUKURU HAJIMETE NO KAWAII DOLL
Original Japanese edition published by KAWADE SHOBO SHINSHA Ltd. Publishers
English translation and production rights arranged with KAWADE SHOBO SHINSHA Ltd.
Publishers through Timo Associates, Inc., Tokyo.
English translation & production rights by World Book Media, LLC, USA

Photography: Nobuhiro Miyoshi (STUDIO60)
Styling: Makiko Iwasaki
Design: Satoko Iwanaga
Process Text (p. 53): Noriko Takai
Illustrations: WADE
Editor: Chie Muramatsu (Cre-Sea)
English Translation: Kyoko Matthews
English Editor: Kerry Bogert

The contents of this book are for personal use only. Patterns herein may be reproduced
in limited quantities for such use. Any large-scale commercial reproduction is prohibited
without the written consent of the publisher. We have made every effort to ensure the
accuracy and completeness of these instructions. We cannot, however, be responsible
for human error, typographical mistakes, or variations in individual work.

British Library Cataloguing in Publication Information available

ISBN 978-0-8117-3958-0

Library of Congress Cataloging-in-Publication Data
Library of Congress Control Number: 2020944824

Contents

Introduction

Welcome to my whimsical world of felted dolls. Here, fairies have tea parties and the neighborhood hares love to read. Each character's charm and personality is brought to life with wool fiber, needle, and imagination.

In this book, I share my process for making these unique felted dolls. From expressive faces to hand-stitched shoes, I've broken down the techniques—from head to toe—in a way that makes the process achievable. Whether you're making your first doll or your hundredth, you'll adore the charm my techniques will bring to your projects.

As you work through the steps to make a doll from wool, you'll quickly discover that no two dolls are the same. Each takes on a life of its own. Using thick wires as the frame of the doll, it becomes posable. With a tilt of the head, wave of the hand, or posture at the tea table, your character's unique personality can shine through.

From start to finish, there is great joy to be found each step of the way.

I would like to say thank you to my family who encourages my doll making, to the wool store teacher who taught me doll making, to Kama-chan who helped me in different ways, and to all who helped me publish this book.

Mihoko Ueno

Chapter One

Meet the Characters

Each character in this book uses the same basic techniques, yet each one has its own personality. From magical fairies to literate rabbits, storybook rivals to inseparable friends, the possibilities are only limited by your imagination.

Flower Fairy

This sweet garden creature hides among the hydrangeas. With her blooming dress, she easily blends into the flowers. Her sky blue wings help her float from plant to plant gathering bouquets of tiny buds.

Instructions, page 64.

Mermaid

You can find this mermaid swimming in a lagoon, gathering seashells for her crown. She stops her search from time to time to talk to the turtles and the crabs she encounters. Just as shell collecting takes time, so will making and stitching the scales of her tail. It's a rewarding task that's worth the effort.

Instructions, page 68.

Red Riding Hood & the Wolf

Wrapped in her woolen hooded cape, Red Riding Hood takes a basket of goodies to her Granny. While wandering through the woods, she meets a charming wolf. With a toothy grin, he offers her a flower in exchange for something from her basket. Red is smart and clever; she won't be fooled by the wolf's tricks.

Instructions, pages 72 and 78.

Reading Friends

You can find these book-loving friends passing the hours together reading under the shade of an old oak tree. From pirates at sea to knights storming a castle, adventure books are their favorite. Neither one wants to leave the other when they're called home for supper.

Instructions, pages 82 and 86.

Librarian

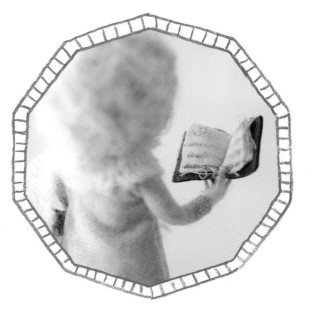

Bundled up in tall winter boots, a hand-knit hat and scarf, and woolen dress, this librarian carries her bag full of books through the snow to the library. She hardly notices the flurries while lost in a good book as she walks.

Instructions, page 90.

Cindy & Her Teddy Bear

Cindy and her teddy bear are an inseparable pair. They snuggle each other tight when they're scared and they laugh out loud when they hear silly things. They're comforted knowing they always have each other.

Instructions, page 94.

Chapter Two

Felting Basics

Before starting your first doll, it's important to get to know the tools and materials you'll be working with, along with a few of the basic techniques used in felting. A strong foundation in these basics will help you as you work to create unique characters with charm and personality.

Tools

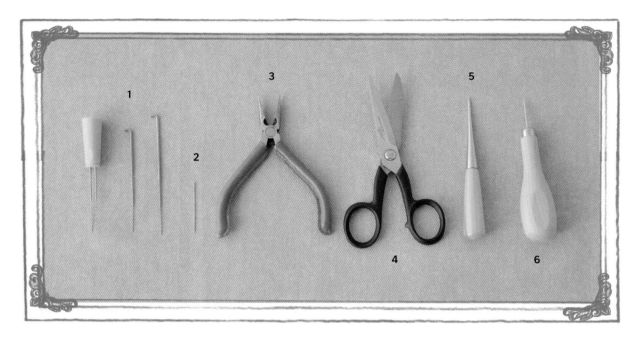

The tools needed to create felted dolls aren't complicated, but they aren't likely to be items you have on hand. Those specifically designed for dimensional felting can be purchased at your local craft supply store or online.

To make the various dolls and accessories in this book, you'll need the following:

(1) Felting Needles

There are several types of needles used in needle felting. What makes them different from other needles is a "barbed" end that works the wool fibers together. Two types of felting needles are shown here. The first (far left) is a dual-needle with an ultra fine tip. Second (middle and right) are standard felting needles. Look for one with an "ultra-fine" tip and one with a "regular" tip.

(2) Sewing Needle

You'll need a standard sewing needle for stitching the clothing your doll will wear. Look for one with a sharp tip to make hand sewing easier.

(3) Chain Nose Pliers

These small pliers can typically be found in the jewelry-making area of a craft store. You'll use them to bend and shape wire when building the body of your doll. Look for a pair with a built-in wire cutter to make cutting the wire easier.

(4) Scissors

A pair of sharp fabric scissors are a must when making doll clothes.

(5) Stiletto

Metal stilettos are used to make holes in your projects. You'll use this when connecting the head to the body.

(6) Awl

With a finer tip than a stiletto, an awl with a sharp point is used to make small holes in small items before they're stitched together. For example, you'll use an awl to punch holes in leather to tie the laces of shoes.

Foam Mat

You'll also need a foam mat to avoid breaking the needle and to protect your work surface when felting.

Materials

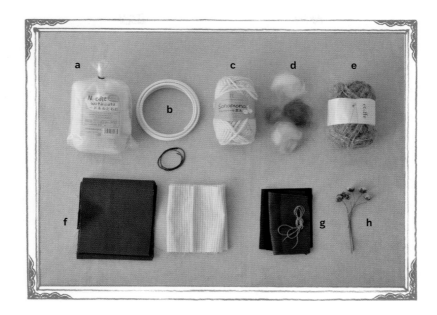

Like the tools used to make the dolls in this book, the materials needed can be found at your local craft supply store or favorite online craft retailer.

Choose colors that speak to your own style or use the natural colors and fabrics shared here for traditional, heirloom-style dolls.

(a) Wool Batt

The wool stuffing used to fill teddy bears is perfect for felting. Combed batt will also work well for needle felting. Be sure you're purchasing 100% natural wool fibers, not synthetic stuffing. Polyester fiber filling will not felt.

(b) Wire

In this book, vinyl coated wire is used to create the posable body of your felted doll. Look for wire that is 8-gauge (3.2 mm) and 12-gauge (2 mm) in thickness. You can also use "craft wire" if stainless steel or coated wires aren't available.

(c) Alpaca Yarn

Other natural fibers like alpaca can be used for the core of the doll's body.

(d) Wool Roving

Dyed wool roving works well for the eyes, mouth, cheeks, and other details of your doll that need a bit of color.

(e) Textured Wool Yarn

Look for textured wool yarns with plied colors (two or more colors twisted together), slubbing (little lumps in the yarn), or other interesting treatments for hair.

(f) Light-Weight Fabrics

You'll use light-weight fabric to make the clothes for your characters. Quilting cotton is affordable and comes in a wide range of colors and patterns.

(g) Felt Sheet and Embroidery Floss

Pre-made wool felt sheets are a great way to make shoes and other small accessories to accompany your doll. You can embellish these mini-makes with embroidery floss.

(h) Miniature Accessories

Keep an eye out at your local craft store and other shops for cute miniature accessories. Small flowers and other objects will go a long way in adding to your doll's personality.

Wool Yarns

For the Body: Worsted-weight yarn (left) is wrapped around the inner framework of the body's core. A single strand of plied, DK-weight yarn (right) is used for articulated fingers.

For Hair: Any weight, color, or textured wool yarn can be used for doll hair. (See *Hairstyles*, pg. 35.)

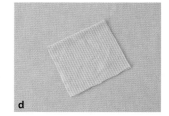

Fabric

(a) Heavy-weight wool fabric works well for doll pants, coats, and other sturdy accessories.

(b) Light-weight wool fabric is a great choice for skirts, sweaters, and other cold weather clothing.

(c) Linen fabric is best for summertime accessories and clothing such as light-weight dresses.

(d) Knit fabric has significant stretch to it and works well for fitted items such as tee shirts.

Felket

This is a specialty Japanese wool product that is a light-weight version of felt sheets found in the US. See *How to Wet Felt* on pg. 22 for tips on making your own.

Leather

Leather scraps are used to make small accessories and shoes for handmade dolls. Choose a thin-weight leather for easier sewing.

Miniature Accessories

Miniature accessories found at craft stores or online craft retailers will add more charm to your handmade dolls. Stores that sell dollhouse accessories are also a great source of miniatures. Here are a few items to look for.

Tin Goods

Tin goods like a miniature mailbox can be used to enhance your doll's environment.

Hats

Doll-sized hats add to your character's personality.

Artificial Flowers

Small flowers become doll-sized bouquets or hair accessories .

Miniature Baskets

You can also make small baskets.
See pg. 61.

Small Branches

Used for making fishing poles or butterfly nets. Choose appropriate thickness and length as needed.

Miniature Buckets

Show your doll's decor style with rustic or painted objects.

Charms

Jewelry charms are the perfect size for handmade dolls.

Bags

Characters can carry their accessories, such as books, with miniature bags and totes.

Small Stones or Shells

Make tiny crowns or trinkets with small stones or shells and wire.

How to Needle Felt

Needle felting is an easy technique that takes practice to get just right. The more you work with wool and learn the way it reacts to the needle, the sooner you'll be on your way to making beautiful one-of-a-kind felt dolls.

To begin your adventure in needle felting, we'll start by making a simple felted ball. Take a baseball size clump of wool stuffing and roll it in your hand to start to form a ball.

Once a ball starts to form, you'll introduce your needle to the process. Work on a foam mat to protect your needle from breaking on a hard surface. **(Fig. 1)**

Hold the needle upright, and then begin stabbing the needle up and down into the fiber ball. **(Fig. 2)** Begin to rotate the ball while continuing to stab the needle up and down.

If stabbing from an angle, be mindful not to bend your needle. It should always go straight into the center of the wool ball. **(Fig. 3)**

Your felted ball is complete when you have a tight, dense sphere.

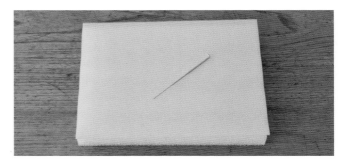

Fig. 1 Needle felting should be done on a foam mat to avoid breaking the needle.

Fig. 2 Hold the needle upright as you stab up and down to form a sphere.

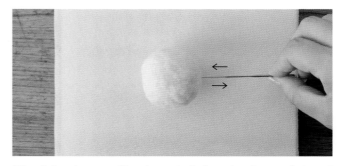

Fig. 3 Continue needling the entire ball moving the needle in and out, side to side. Be careful not to bend the needle as you work.

How to Blend Colors

One of the beautiful qualities of wool fibers is their ability to be blended. If you look very closely at some commercially dyed yarns, you may notice that many colors make up the solid color you see.

This means that you aren't limited to the palette of wool you have on hand. You can make additional colors by simply blending them.

In the example shown here, blue and white wool are blended together to create light blue. This is a very simple technique that can be used to make your felted characters one-of-a-kind.

Gather small tufts of blue and white wool roving. Each piece should be approximately the same size. **(Fig. 4)** Hold the pieces so the colors run parallel to each other to form a two-tone length of wool.

Next, holding each end of the lengths of roving, gently pull in opposite directions to divide the lengths in half. Lay the two piece on top of one another and gently pull them apart again. **(Fig. 5)**

Continue layering and pulling the fibers until the colors blend to light blue. **(Fig. 6)** If you look closely, you'll see the individually colored fibers. However, when looking from a normal viewing distance, the colors meld together into light blue.

Fig. 4 Begin with two different colors of wool roving approximately the same size.

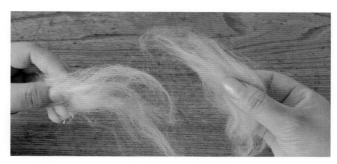

Fig. 5 Hold the pieces at either end and gently pull them apart. Layer them again and repeat.

Fig. 6 Continue pulling the fibers, layering them, and pulling again until the new color is achieved.

How to Wet Felt

Felket is a Japanese wool fiber sheet that is similar to the felt sheet found in the U.S. However, where the American felt sheet is dense and stiff, felket is light weight and somewhat flimsy. Wet felting felket will further felt the fiber into a denser fabric.

The materials needed to wet felt are:

- Felket or other thin felt sheet
- Shallow container of soapy water

- Bubble wrap
- Protective gloves

If you aren't able to locate felket or thin felt sheet in your area, you can create your own using wool roving! Simply pull wool roving into tufts as you would to blend colors. Then, lay the fiber tufts side by side in a shallow tray. Make sure the fiber tufts are aligned in rows and all going in the same direction. Add a second layer of tufts going in the opposite direction to the first. If thicker felt sheet is desired, you can layer more wool tufts. Cover the wool tufts with a piece of tulle or polyester fabric. Add a solution of warm water and dish soap, then follow the steps outlined for felket shown here.

The Flower Fairy's wings are made using thin felt sheet. See page 64.

1. Place felket in a shallow tray and pour warm soapy water to cover.

2. Fully submerge the fiber until completely soaked with water.

3. Rub the surface evenly, agitating the fiber back and forth.

4. Transfer the felket to a piece of bubble wrap and start to roll it up.

5. Once fully rolled, unroll and then reroll the bubble wrap and fiber. Repeat this rolling and unrolling several times.

6. After felting, pinch the surface. If the surface rises up together, it is done. Rinse with clean water and dry. If the wool comes apart, repeat Steps 3-5 until fully felted.

Chapter Three

Making a Felted Doll

The method used to make each unique felted doll starts with the same few steps; make and shape the head, embellish the face, and then create and attach the body. Choices you make along the way give your doll its own personality. Eye color, rosy cheeks, and hairstyles are a few of the features you can customize as you go.

Part 1

Making & Embellishing the Head

Take your time when making your doll's head. Each feature is a way to give your doll its own unique personality. Slight changes make all the difference when it comes to facial expressions.

Head

1. Roll 7 to 8 grams of wool batt or stuffing into a ball.

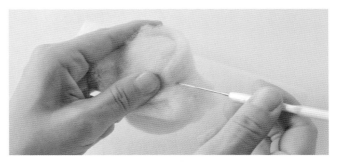

2. Use a regular-tipped felting needle to start forming the fibers into a tight, dense sphere.

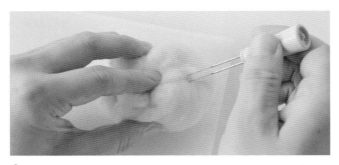

3. Change to an ultra-fine dual needle and keep stabbing to make a firm ball shape.

4. Work until the finished size is about 1¾ in (4.5 cm) in diameter.

TIP

Listen to Your Felting

If you listen carefully as you're felting the wool, you'll hear the sound become quiet and smooth when you're nearly finished.

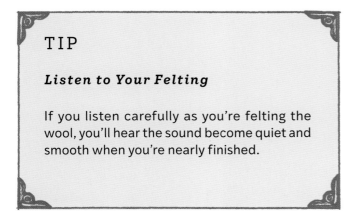

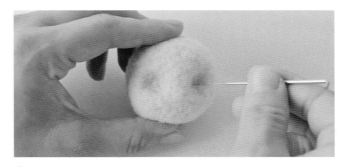

5. Using an ultra-fine single needle, make dents for eyes.

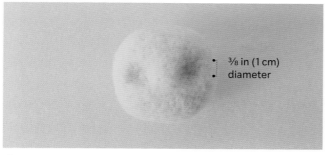

6. When finished, the eye sockets should be about ⅜ in (1 cm) from top to bottom.

⅜ in (1 cm) diameter

7. Continuing with the same needle, stab the outline of the nose.

8. When finished, the nose creates a U-shape from eye to eye.

9. Create the look of cheekbones by needling along the sides of the face with a dual needle.

TIP

Use your fingers to press and mold the face as you go.

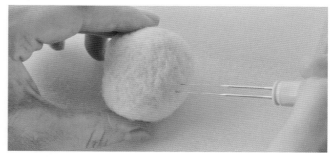

10. Using a dual needle, shape the back of the head, forming a slight indent at the base of the skull.

Progress Check

After Step 10, the back of the head should have a smooth round shape. This is best viewed looking at the profile of the head.

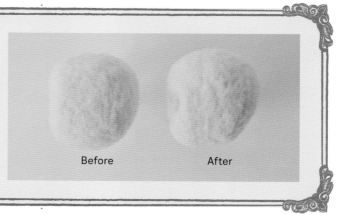

Before   After

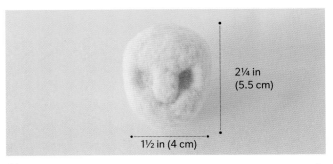

2¼ in (5.5 cm)

1½ in (4 cm)

11. The head and face should measure approximately 2¼ x 1½ in (5.5 x 4 cm).

12. Continue to needle the features of the face to soften and refine the jawline, cheeks, and nose. Stab the area under the nose so it's firm.

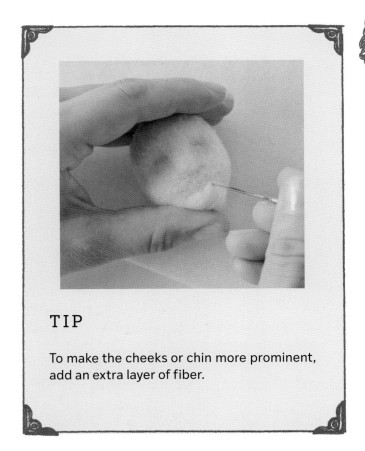

TIP

To make the cheeks or chin more prominent, add an extra layer of fiber.

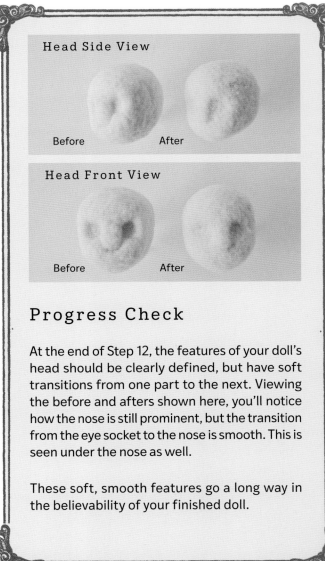

Head Side View

Before   After

Head Front View

Before   After

Progress Check

At the end of Step 12, the features of your doll's head should be clearly defined, but have soft transitions from one part to the next. Viewing the before and afters shown here, you'll notice how the nose is still prominent, but the transition from the eye socket to the nose is smooth. This is seen under the nose as well.

These soft, smooth features go a long way in the believability of your finished doll.

Eyes & Mouth

13. Using an ultra-fine needle, add a small amount of wool roving into the eye socket. Natural tone roving will make the color of eye stand out and stops the color from blurring at the edges.

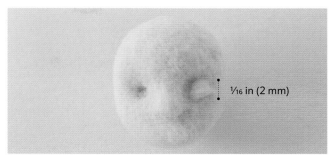

1/16 in (2 mm)

14. The eyeball added should be approximately 1/16 in (2 mm). Add the second eye in the same way.

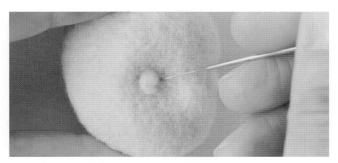

15. Continue to refine the eyes, forming a crisp edge around the eyeballs.

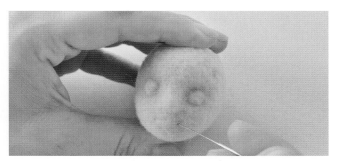

16. Using an ultra-fine needle, attach the mouth temporarily. Twist a small amount of pink roving into fine string and stab in a line.

TIP

The left eye was made with a natural tone roving eyeball underneath the blue roving, while the right was made without. Taking the time to add the natural tone roving underneath allows the color to stand out and creates a nicer finish.

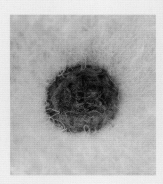
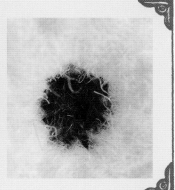

17. With an ultra-fine needle, add color for the eyes on top of the eyeballs. Stab the edge of the eyes first, then stab the inside area. Stab the center of the eyes several times to shape.

18. To give the eyes more depth, add a small layer of a different color of wool. Here two shades of blue wool are used. Repeat for the second eye.

Final Shaping

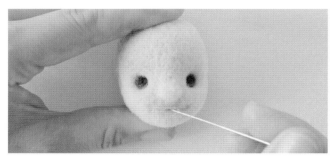

19. When the eyes are complete, focus on shaping the mouth. Needle the center lip line deeply to form an upper and lower lip.

20. Continue to refine the shape of the forehead and face as needed.

21. Further shape the cheekbones as needed.

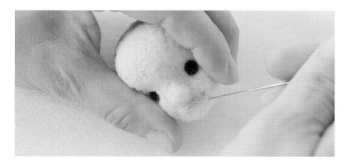

22. Adjust the lower jawline and chin.

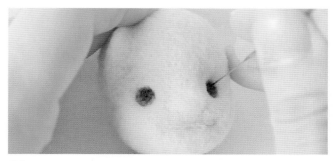

23. With an ultra-fine needle, make sure the eyes are parallel on the face. Using a stabbing motion, move them if needed.

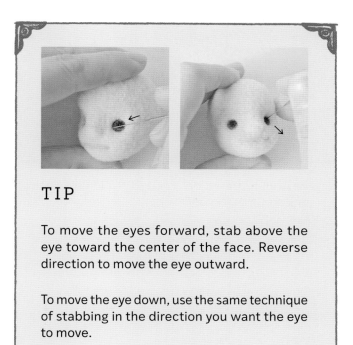

TIP

To move the eyes forward, stab above the eye toward the center of the face. Reverse direction to move the eye outward.

To move the eye down, use the same technique of stabbing in the direction you want the eye to move.

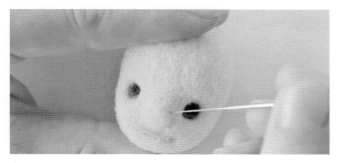

24. Adjust the shape of the nose as needed to give the center bridge some height.

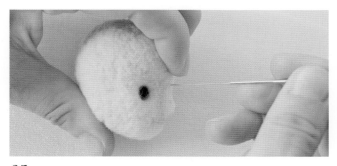

25. Stab from above the tip of the nose to between the eyebrows to further shape.

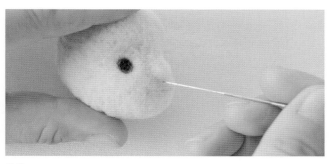

26. Stab under the nose to define the bottom edge.

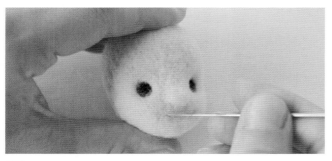

27. Stab 2 to 3 times, back and forth along the line of the mouth.

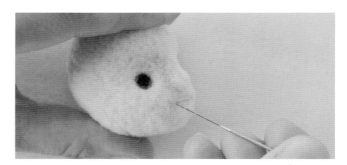

28. Stab another 2 to 3 times as you insert the needle from below at a 30-degree angle.

TIP

If you stab the needle in at a 90-degree angle, the mouth will sink in and you'll end up with a droopy expression.

29. When complete, the mouth will have upper and lower lips separated by a fine pink line.

Progress Check

As you work each step to refine and define various areas of the face, the head becomes more compact and realistic. As seen here, before working Steps 23-29, the head appears soft and undefined. You're on the right track when your head resembles the examples showing the after effects.

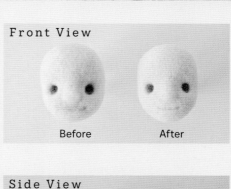

Front View

Before   After

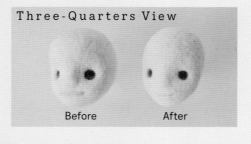

Three-Quarters View

Before   After

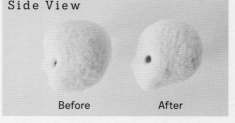

Side View

Before   After

Finishing Touches

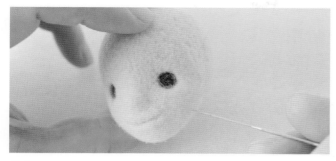

30. For rosy cheeks, mix 2 or 3 shades of pink wool. Place the blended wool on the cheek temporarily and stab lightly.

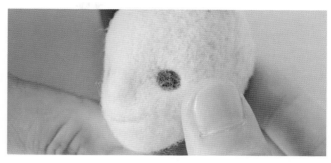

31. Rub the cheek with your thumb to blend the color.

32. Trim excess fiber with scissors.

33. To add ears, gather a small ball of wool.

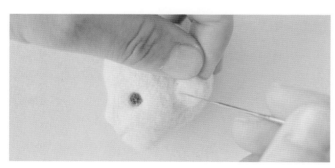

34. Using an ultra-fine needle, attach the ball of wool to the side of the head.

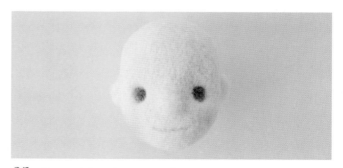

35. Repeat for the second ear.

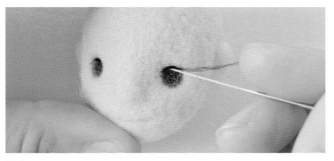

36. To emphasize the eyes, add a thin strand of wool roving as eyeliner at the top edge of the eyes.

37. To emphasize the rosy cheeks, add a layer of brighter pink roving at the center of each cheek.

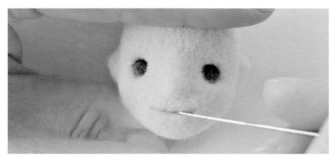

38. To add lipstick, stab darker pink wool along the bottom lip.

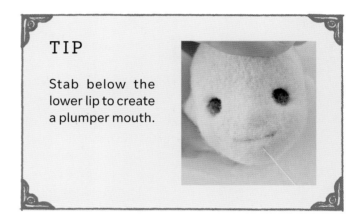

TIP

Stab below the lower lip to create a plumper mouth.

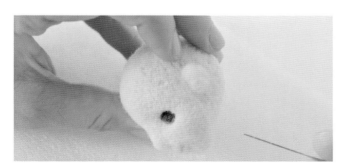

39. If you find any needle holes in your doll's head, stab the surrounding areas lightly to close the gaps.

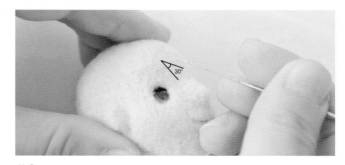

40. To smooth any rough areas of skin, stab the needle in at a 30-degree angle, not straight down.

Hairstyles

With the head of your doll complete, it's time to add hair. There is no limit to the number of ways you can style your doll's hair, but how you attach it to the head is the same, no matter the style.

Attaching Hair

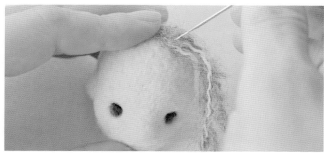

1. Cut several lengths of yarn about 25 in (64 cm) long and fold 3 or 4 times. Gather and stab the folded yarn ends to the top of the head.

2. With an ultra-fine needle, stab yarn to both the right side and left side of the head. Continue adding yarn to cover the crown of the head.

3. After adding the hair, trim the ends to your preferred length.

4. To style the hair into a short bob, trim the ends to the approximate length shown in Step 3. Then use your finger to curl the hair under.

5. Using an ultra-fine needle, stab the ends of the folded strands to the head.

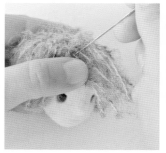

6. Trim the yarn to create bangs and stab to the head.

Hairstyle Options

Yarns

Use any wool or wool tweed yarn to achieve the hairstyles shown. If the yarn is plied (more than one strand twisted together), untwist the plies before attaching to the head.

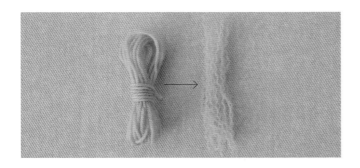

Long Hair   Braids

Long hair parted down the center.

Long hair parted down one side.

Long hair with various lengths of wool to create a carefree style.

Braid long hairstyles and finish with a small bow or ribbon to hold in place.

Chignon

Chignon with lots of volume.

Chignon with a tight, smooth finish.

1. Add yarn with the hair flowing toward the back of the head.

2. Add hair along the edges of the head, then collect the strands together into a ponytail and secure with a piece of yarn.

3. Twist and shape into a bun, trim excess yarn.

4. Add a swoop of bangs and tie a ribbon around the bun to finish.

Teased hair with lots of volume.

Teased hair with woolen spun yarn.

Teased hair cut to various short lengths.

1. Short, single strands of yarn added all over the head create a teased look. Stab the center of a single, short strand of yarn.

2. Repeat Step 1 to cover the top of the head.

3. Add hair to the sides of the head.

4. Continue adding more hair until desired volume is achieved.

Short Hair

Short hair with bangs cut above the eyebrows.

Short hair cut to one length.

1. Here, shorter lengths of untwisted yarn are felted to the head.

2. The yarn is added to the entire head. Once bangs are added, the hair is then cut to chin length.

Very Short Hair

Very short hair styled close to the head.

1. Add short lengths of yarn to the head.

2. Fold the yarn against the head and needle felt in place. Do not cut the yarn. Continue folding it onto itself and needle felt in place.

Part 3

Making the Body

A basic body for your doll will be made using wire, yarn, and wool batt or stuffing. You can take things a step further with more complex elements like posable fingers.

Wire Frame

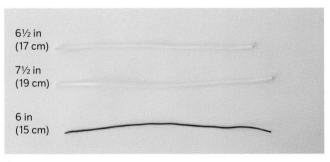

6½ in (17 cm)

7½ in (19 cm)

6 in (15 cm)

1. The body is made by wrapping a wire frame in yarn and fiber. Cut a 6½ in (17 cm) and a 7½ in (19 cm) piece of 8-gauge wire for the body. Cut a 6 in (15 cm) piece of 12-gauge wire for the arms.

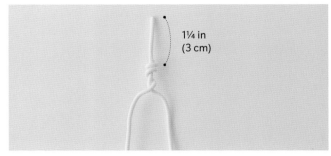

1¼ in (3 cm)

2. Coil the shorter 8-gauge wire around the longer wire a few times, leaving about 1¼ in (3 cm) for the body.

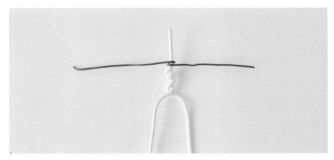

3. Coil the 12-gauge wire around the body to form arms.

1

1

4. Make a hole at the bottom of the head and insert the wire frame. The head and center of the body should be about equal in size (head:body = 1:1).

Body

5. With the head in place, wrap the center of the wire frame with wool batt or stuffing.

6. Remove the head and wrap the wool batt with worsted weight wool yarn. First, make a few vertical wraps, and then wrap horizontally.

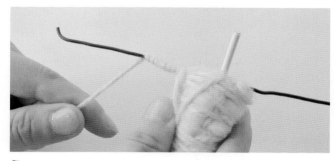

7. Continue wrapping the yarn down the arm. Leave 1¼ in (3 cm) of the wire exposed for the hand and wrap back toward the center. Wrap the other arm the same way.

8. Wrap yarn down and back up each leg. Leave 1¼ in (3 cm) of exposed wire at the end similar to the arms.

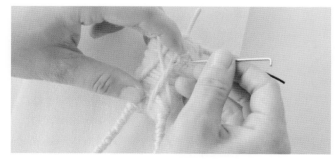

9. Continue to wrap yarn around the body, then use a regular tip needle to begin felting the yarn to the core.

10. Add a layer of wool batt to the body and needle felt.

11. Place the head back on the frame. Check that the body is balanced and not heavier on one side than the other.

12. Add wool batt to the shoulders and felt with a regular tip needle.

Arms

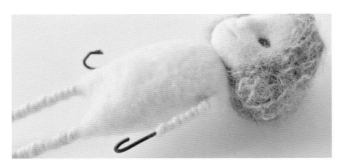

13. Determine the length of the arms. The exposed wire should reach the thigh area of the leg. Use pliers to curl the wire ends.

14. Wrap wool batt around the exposed wire of the arm, leaving about ⅜ in (1 cm) still exposed.

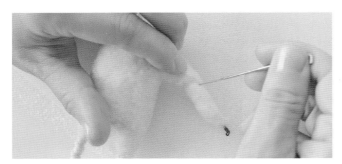

15. Using an ultra-fine needle, felt the wool batt on the arm until well attached.

16. Slide wool of the arm away from the hand area and cut the wire, removing about ⅝ in (1.5 cm).

Basic Hands & Fingers

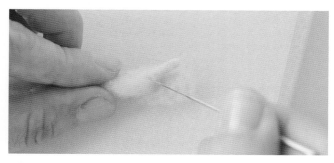

17. Slide the fiber that was pushed back in Step 16 down the arm. The area without a wire core will become a hand. Using an ultra-fine needle, stab the hand area to flatten it out.

18. Make a thumb with wool batt and felt it to the hand with an ultra-fine needle. This creates a mitten-shaped hand.

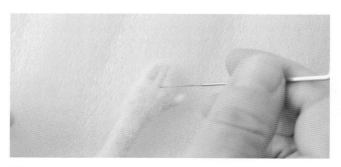

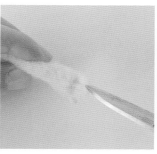

19. Add three lines to separate the large portion of the hand into four fingers.

20. Using sharp scissors, cut the line dividing each finger. Needle felt individual fingers as needed to adjust the shape.

21. Once finished, the hand will have four fingers and a thumb.

Posable Fingers

Creating hands with fingers that can be bent and shaped to hold objects is more challenging than basic hands, but you'll find they're well worth the effort.

Note: You can make any doll in this book with either style hand. Whichever style you choose to make is entirely up to you.

1. Cut five 2 in (5 cm) long pieces of 28-gauge stainless steel wire. Untwist a piece of DK-weight yarn to prepare five 6 in (15 cm) long strands.

2. Wrap the yarn around the wire, covering about ⅜ in (1 cm). Leave the tip of the wire exposed.

3. Use pliers to bend the exposed end of wire against the area wrapped with yarn.

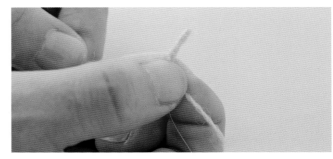

4. Continue wrapping until the finger reaches desired thickness, taking care to cover the bent wire from Step 3. Repeat Steps 2-4 to make a total of five fingers for each hand.

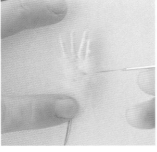

5. Twist the wires of four fingers together and leave a gap between fingers. Wrap wool batt around the twisted wires to make the palm of the hand. Felt with an ultra-fine needle.

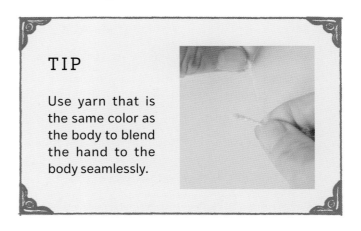

TIP

Use yarn that is the same color as the body to blend the hand to the body seamlessly.

6. Add the remaining piece of wire to create the thumb. Twist the thumb wire around the base of the palm. Add more wool batt and felt in place.

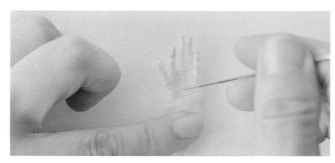

7. Add more wool batt to the palm as needed and felt in place.

8. Wrap wool batt around the base of the finger wires to form a wrist and felt in place. Repeat for the second hand.

9. Using the length of the wrist just made as a guide, trim the excess arm wire.

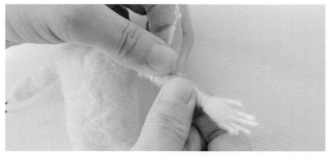

10. Wrap a strand of DK-weight wool yarn around the wrist and arm to connect the two components.

11. Cover the yarn with wool batt and felt with an ultra-fine needle. Repeat to attach the second hand.

Legs & Feet

22. Trim excess leg wires to about ¼ in (5 mm) longer than the area wrapped with yarn. Bend the exposed wire back against the leg.

23. Wrap the legs with wool batt.

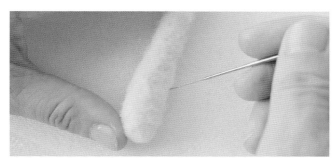

24. Using an ultra-fine needle, stab the wool batt until desired thickness of the leg is achieved.

25. Bend leg wire at the ankle area to make a foot. The foot should be about ¾-1 in (2-2.5 cm) long.

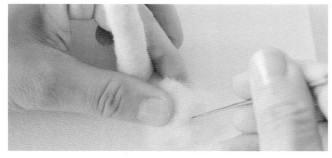

26. Add extra wool batt to the top of the foot and to the toes. Needle felt to fully attach.

27. Add extra wool batt to the back of the foot to fully form the heel.

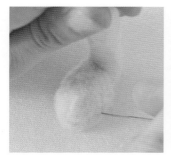

28. With the doll in a standing position, stab the foot from the top down to form a flat sole.

TIP

For the doll to stand on its own, it's helpful to slightly bend the legs at the knees. This adjusts the center of gravity and helps balance the doll. This balance may change once clothing is added, so adjust as needed after dressing.

Part 4

Sewing Clothes & Shoes

Each character in this book has a unique wardrobe, but the methods used to sew the garments and shoes are the same throughout. In this section, we will sew a simple dress, pants, and basic shoes to outline the process.

Basic Dress

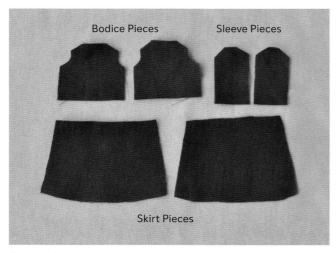

Bodice Pieces   Sleeve Pieces

Skirt Pieces

1. From a piece of wool fabric about 8 x 12 in (20 x 30 cm), cut two pieces for the bodice, two pieces for the sleeve, and two pieces for the skirt as shown.

Note: Every doll is unique, so standard pattern pieces are not available. Cut pieces in the approximate shape shown in a size to fit your doll.

Bodice   Sleeve Pieces

2. Align the front and back bodice pieces with right sides together, and sew shoulder and side seams.

Note: Contrasting thread is used to highlight the area sewn throughout. You'll want to sew your dress with thread that matches the fabric.

3. For ease of fitting, remove the doll's head. With right sides out, put the bodice on the body.

4. Attach the sleeves. Fold the cuff end of the sleeve toward the wrong side about ¼ in (5 mm). Wrap the sleeve around the arm and stitch the sleeve seam.

5. Sew the sleeve to the armhole of the bodice.

6. Align the two skirt pieces with right sides together, and sew the side seams.

7. Turn the skirt right side out. Fold about ¼ in (5 mm) of the waist of the skirt toward the wrong side and sew with running stitch to gather.

8. Align the skirt waist with the bottom of the bodice. Pull the thread of the running stitch to gather the skirt waist to fit.

9. Sew the skirt to the bodice, then remove the running stitch.

10. Fold the hem of the skirt to the wrong side and sew in place with hem stitch. When finished, reattach the head to the dress. Position the head to fully cover the neckline. Affix the head with glue, if needed.

Pants & Shorts

◆ ◆

Note: Full length pants and shorts use the same technique.

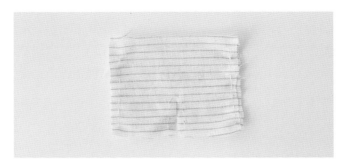

11. Cut two rectangles from light-weight linen fabric. Cut a slit in the center of each piece. Align the two pieces with right sides together, sew the side seams and crotch as shown.

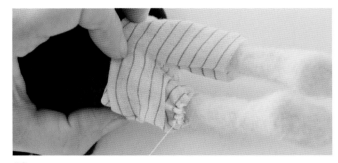

12. Turn the shorts right side out and put them on the doll. Fold the hem of each pant leg toward the wrong side and sew running stitch to gather. Do the same to gather the waist. Secure the gathers with a knot.

Shoes

◆ ◆

Note: The various styles of shoes shown in this book follow the same construction method. Shown here is a short, laced boot made with wool fabric.

13. Using your doll's feet as a guide to the size of pieces needed, cut out a tongue, body, toe, and sole for each shoe from wool fabric or felt sheet.

    Note: Contrasting thread is shown throughout to make the stitched seams visible. Use coordinating thread when sewing your shoes.

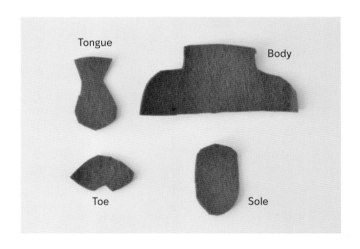

Tongue

Body

Toe

Sole

14. Place the tongue of the shoe on the top of the foot with the rounded end up. Wrap the body of the shoe around the foot. Stitch the toe together with mattress stitch.

15. Adhere the toe piece to the shoe with glue, positioning with the notched side toward the sole. Bring the points of the notch together and hold in place until secure.

16. Using two sewing needles and thread, sew from the toe toward the ankle, crossing at the center, to create laces. Tie a bow at the ankle and trim the excess thread.

17. Glue the sole to the bottom of the foot.

18. Use scissors to trim the sole to fit the outline of the upper shoe.

19. Repeat Steps 14-18 for the second shoe.

20. The boots seen here were made with leather and do not use a tongue or toe piece. The body pieces are made to wrap around the entire ankle and leg. They can be made short (top) or tall (bottom).

Cindy wears a basic wool dress, striped shorts, and laced boots.

Personifying an Animal

Storybook characters and garden friends come to life using the same techniques as other felted dolls. Standing on two feet, with clothes and accessories, their charm and whimsy are on full display.

Head & Face

Note: Personified animals begin with the same basic steps as a human doll. (See Making a Felted Doll, *pg. 25.) The face is worked on an egg-shaped ball to create the muzzle.*

1. Following Steps 1-4 of Part 1: Making & Embellishing the Head (pg. 26), use 6-7 grams of wool batt or stuffing to make an egg-shaped head.

2. With an ultra-fine needle, stab a line of brown roving to form the nose.

3. Continue the brown roving down from the nose to form the mouth.

4. Continuing with an ultra-fine needle, shape the areas around the nose and mouth.

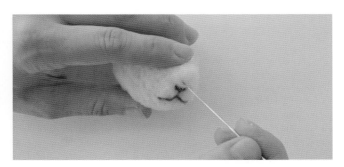

5. Add extra wool batt to the area above the nose to give it more dimension.

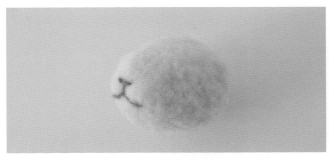

6. The area above the nose should be raised slightly.

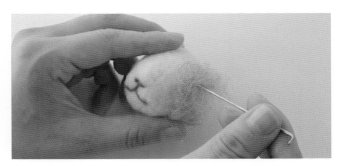

7. Needle felt gray wool roving to the entire head, leaving the nose and mouth area natural.

8. Stab as you fill the spaces little by little.

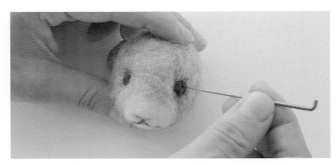

9. Following Steps 5-6 and 13-23 of Part 1: Making & Embellishing the Head (pgs. 26-27 and 29-31), make the eye sockets and eyeballs, and add the eye color.

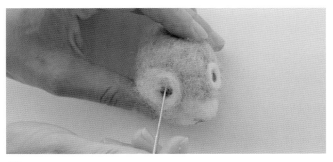

10. Using an ultra-fine needle, add a ring of white wool roving around the eyes.

11. The head and face are complete.

Ears

* *

12. Wet felt gray fiber into a sheet, then cut two ear pieces. Repeat with white felt sheet for the two inner ear pieces. (See *How to Wet Felt,* pg. 22.)

13. With an ultra-fine needle, felt a white inner ear piece to a gray ear piece. Repeat for the second ear.

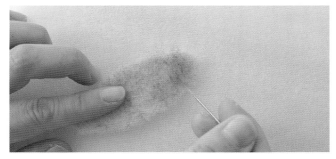

14. Add a small amount of black wool roving to the tip of the back of the ear.

15. Repeat Step 14 to add black wool to the tip of the front of the ear in the same way.

16. Attach the ear to the head. Bring the bottom corners of the ear together, with the inner ear turned outward, and needle felt the bottom area to the head. Repeat for the second ear.

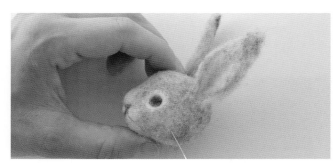

17. With an ultra-fine needle, add a small amount of pink wool roving to the cheeks.

Body

◆ ◆

18. The animal head is complete.

19. Using gray wool batt and yarn, follow the steps outlined in Part 3: Making the Body (pgs. 40-42) to create the animal's body.

20. Follow Steps 17 and 18 (pg. 43) to make mitten-shaped hands. Do not divide the hand to make fingers.

21. Follow Steps 22-28 (pgs. 46-47) to form the feet and position the animal to stand.

Part 6

Small Accessories

Add interesting details and enhance your doll's persona with miniature accessories. Hand-knit hats, scarves, felted toy animals, and more, make your doll unique and develop their personality.

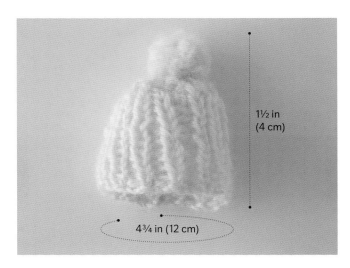

1½ in (4 cm)

4¾ in (12 cm)

Tools & Materials

- U.S. size 0 (2 mm) double-pointed knitting needles
- Tapestry needle
- Fingering weight (#1, superfine) yarn

Abbreviations

- **k** knit
- **p** purl
- **k2tog** knit 2 stitches together
- **sts** stitches

Note: The size of your doll's hat changes depending on the thickness of yarn and size of needles you choose. You may need to experiment to get just the right fit.

Hand Knit Hat

Instructions

Row 1: Cast on 24 sts, join for knitting in the round.

Rounds 2-10: K1, p1 around.

Round 11: [K2tog, (k1, p1) 3 times] around. 21 sts.

Round 12: [K2tog, (p1, k1) 2 times, p1] around. 18 sts.

Round 13: [K2tog, (k1, p1) 2 times] around. 15 sts.

Round 14: [K2tog, p1, k1, p1] around. 12 sts.

Break the yarn leaving a tail about 12 in (30 cm) long. Thread the tail onto a tapestry needle and pass the needle though the remaining stitches. Pull the tail to close the top of the hat. Weave in tail.

Pom-Pom

1. Wrap yarn around 1 in (2.5 cm) piece of cardboard 10 times.

2. Slide the wrapped yarn off the cardboard and secure with a knot around the center.

3. Cut the loops of the wrapped yarn and shape pom-pom into a ball.

4. Sew the pom-pom to the top of the hat.

1 in (2.5 cm)

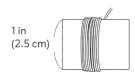

Width 1 in (2.5 cm)
Length 9 in (23 cm)

Tools & Materials

- U.S. size 0 (2 mm) double-pointed or straight knitting needles
- U.S. size 2 (2 mm) steel crochet hook
- Tapestry needle
- Fingering weight (#1, superfine) yarn

Abbreviations

- **k** knit
- **p** purl
- **k2tog** knit 2 stitches together
- **sts** stitches

Note: The size of your doll's scarf changes depending on the thickness of yarn and size of needles you choose. You may need to experiment to get just the right size.

Hand Knit Scarf

Instructions

Row 1: Cast on 11 sts.

Row 2, and all even rows: (P1, k1) across, p1.

Row 3, and all odd rows: (K1, p1) across, k1.

Row 82: Bind off all sts in pattern.

Cut working yarn and weave in tail.

Use the tutorial provided to add fringe to the cast-on and bind-off ends of the scarf.

Fringe

1. Cut 11 pieces of yarn 1½ in (4 cm) long. Fold each piece of yarn in half.

2. Using a steel crochet hook, pull a folded piece of yarn through a stitch. **(Fig. 1)**

3. Pass the cut ends of yarn through the loop pulled through the stitch. Pull the ends away from the scarf to secure. **(Fig. 2)**

4. Repeat Steps 2-3 to add a folded piece of yarn to each cast-on and bind-off stitch.

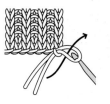

Fig. 1

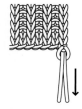

Fig. 2

Stuffed Toys

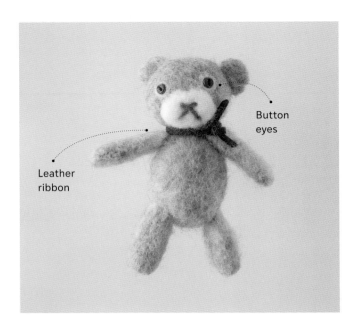

Leather ribbon

Button eyes

Teddy Bear

Instructions

1. Make the head, body, arms, legs, and ears with gray wool batt or stuffing.

2. Add white wool roving to eyes and muzzle.

3. Needle felt an X for the nose and mouth with brown wool roving.

4. Sew buttons for eyes.

5. Add a leather ribbon to the neck.

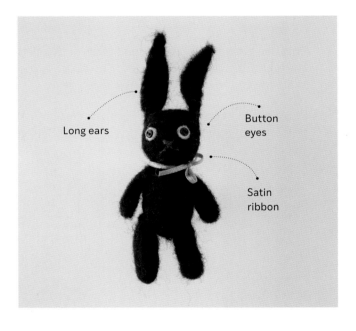

Long ears

Button eyes

Satin ribbon

Stuffed Rabbit

Instructions

1. Make the head, body, arms, and legs with black wool batt or stuffing.

2. Add white wool roving to eyes.

3. Make long ears with felket or felted sheet and attach to head.

4. Needle felt a small nose and mouth with brown wool roving.

5. Sew buttons for eyes.

6. Add a satin ribbon to the neck.

Birds

  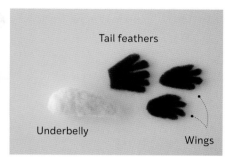

Tail feathers

Underbelly

Wings

Instructions

1. Make the body using wool roving in the color desired.

2. Use felket or felt sheet to make tail feathers, wings, and underbelly. Needle felt the components to the body.

3. Add white wool roving to eyes. Add brown wool roving to the center of the eyes.

4. Make a beak with brown wool roving and attach.

Fruits & Bread

Instructions

Fruit

1. Make apple and pear-shaped felted balls with appropriately colored wool roving.

2. Glue small pieces of wood or heavy-weight thread to make a stem.

Bread

3. Make a loaf-shaped felted ball with brown wool roving.

4. Needle felt lines of dark brown roving on the top of the loaf.

Books

1. Cut a rectangle of leather for the cover of the book and several pieces of linen to act as pages.

2. Use letter stamps and ink to imprint text on the fabric pages of the book. With needle and thread, sew the pages to the leather binding along the center and fold the book closed.

Glasses

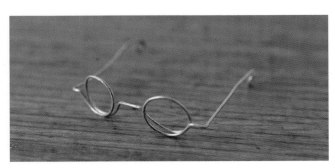

1. Using a pencil and a piece of craft wire about 12 in (30 cm) long, make two loops in the wire to form the rims of the glasses.

2. Use pliers to bend the wire on either side of the rims to form the temples of the frames. Coil the end of each temple into a small loop.

Apple

1. Form white polymer clay into the shape of an apple and set according to manufacturer's instructions. Paint the apple red and allow to dry.

2. Glue a small piece of wood or heavy-weight thread to the apple as a stem.

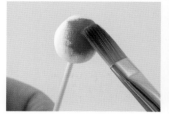

Leather Basket

1. From a piece of leather, cut a side, bottom, and handle for the basket. The side piece should be long enough to wrap the circumference of the bottom piece.

2. Sew short ends of the side piece together to form a loop. Sew the bottom piece to the side piece. Attach the handle.

Bottom

Side

Handle

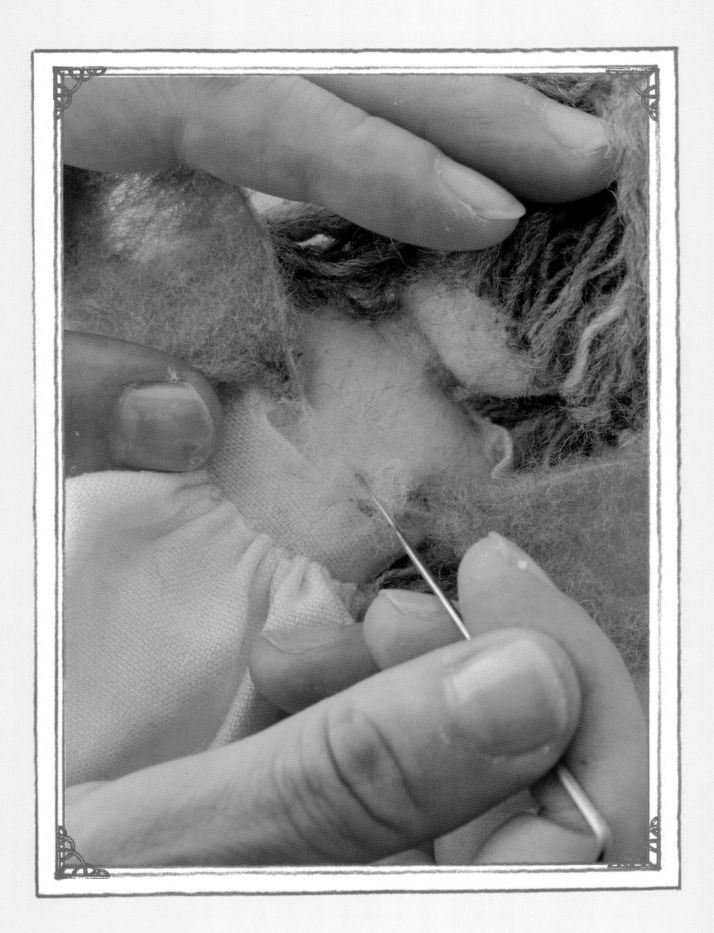

Chapter Four

Making the Characters

The doll designs included in this book will teach you important skills in creating characters that have charm and personality. You can follow my step-by-step instructions here in this chapter, or use the information as a springboard for your own ideas. Your color choices, fabric selections, and posing will tell each character's unique story.

Flower Fairy

Make a whimsical woodland fairy who loves gathering flowers. Her pale blue wings carry her through the forest to your garden gate. She's sure to be a favorite in your felted doll collection.

Finished Size

- 7 in (18 cm) tall

Fibers

- **Head,** 7 g natural wool batt
- **Body,** 3 g natural wool batt
- **Eyes,** 1 g each of navy blue, natural tone, and aqua blue wool roving
- **Mouth,** 1 g each of peach and light brown wool roving
- **Cheeks,** 1 g each of rose, peach, and persimmon, blended wool roving
- **Wings,** blue felket or felt sheet, about 2¾ x 6 in (7 x 15 cm)

Wires

- **Body Core,** about 14¼ in (36 cm) of 8-gauge wire and about 6 in (15 cm) of 12-gauge craft wire
- **Finger Core,** about 19¾ in (50 cm) of 28-gauge wire
- **Wings,** about 12 in (30 cm) of 24-gauge stainless steel wire

Yarns

- **Body Base Yarn,** Sonomono Alpaca Wool; worsted weight, natural colorway (or other worsted-weight alpaca yarn)
- **Fingers,** Sonomono DK; DK weight, natural colorway (or other DK-weight wool yarn)
- **Hair,** plied fingering or worsted-weight yarns in mixed colors, cut desired lengths and untwisted

Fabric

- **Dress,** white linen about 8 x 12 in (20 x 30 cm)

Other

- **Miniature flowers,** 8-10 in various colors
- Sewing thread

Tools

- Felting needles
- Sewing needle
- Chain nose pliers
- Scissors
- Stiletto
- Awl

Hair

Untwist plied yarns with shades of ivory, gray, and brown for long wavy hair.

Flower Fascinator

Sew small flowers in the fairy's hair, securing them to her head.

Hands

Create posable fingers with wired hands.

Feet

Leave this fairy barefoot, exposing her five tiny toes.

Instructions

✦ ◆ ✦

Make the Doll

Referring to the step-by-step instructions in *Making a Felted Doll* (pgs. 26-47), create the Flower Fairy as follows:

1. Make the head with natural color wool batt before embellishing the face. Add eyes using natural color roving in the eye socket, with aqua blue and navy for the eyeball color. Add rosy cheeks with rose, peach, and persimmon colored roving blended together. Add the mouth with peach and light brown fiber.

2. Add hair to the head. Untwist fingering or worsted-weight plied yarn in shades of ivory, gray, and brown. Needle felt the yarn to the head and trim to desired length.

3. Make the body using 8-gauge wire for the core of the body and 12-gauge wire for the legs and arms. The core wires are wrapped in worsted-weight alpaca yarn and then natural color wool batt is needle felted to the core.

4. Once the body is formed, sculpt the arms and legs by needle felting wool batt to the wrapped core wires. Make five toes for the exposed bare feet in the same way as basic fingers are formed (see pg. 43). Use the technique on page 44 to create hands with posable fingers.

5. Temporarily attach the head to the body.

Sew the Clothes

Referring to *Sewing Clothes & Shoes* (pgs. 48-51) as needed, make the Flower Fairy Dress as follows:

6. Using the photo as a guide **(Fig. 1)**, cut the dress pieces from white linen fabric. This fabric does not have stretch, so it will be sewn directly to the doll's body.

Note: Each doll is unique based on the amount of wool batt used to make the body. As a result, pattern pieces cannot be standardized. Pieces should be cut to fit your doll.

7. Make a few clips into the curved neckline on the front body. Fold the raw edge over and hand stitch in place. To finish the neckline on the back body, fold the raw edges over and hand stitch in place as well.

8. Align the front body and the back body pieces with right sides together. Sew the shoulder seams to create the bodice. Adjust the size according to your doll as you go.

9. Remove the doll's head. Place the bodice on the doll, sew the side body seams together and attach the sleeves. Reattach the head.

10. Align short sides of the skirt with right sides together and sew. This seam will become the back center of the skirt. Turn the skirt right side out.

11. Gather the skirt waist and sew it to the dress bodice. You may find it easiest to sew the skirt directly to the doll's body when attaching to the bodice.

12. To hem the dress, fold a scant amount of the bottom of the skirt to the wrong side. Sew running stitch along the hem and gather. **(Fig. 2)** The skirt will have a balloon-like shape once gathered. **(Fig. 3)**

> TIP
>
> If the weight of the fabric causes the skirt to hang low, you can lift the skirt with a few tuck stitches sewn to the inside of the skirt.

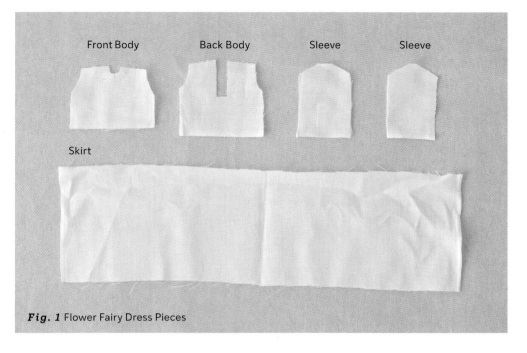

Fig. 1 Flower Fairy Dress Pieces

Front Body   Back Body   Sleeve   Sleeve

Skirt

Fig. 2

Fig. 3

Make the Wings

13. Using 24-gauge stainless steel wire, create two wire wings. Starting in the center of a piece of wire about 12 in (30 cm) long, form the top of the left wing. Then bend the wire to form the bottom of the left wing. Wrap the tail of wire on the left side around the center of the main wire. Do the same to the right side to mirror the left wing. Cut the excess wire when complete. **(Fig. 4)**

14. Cut two pieces of felket or felt sheet that has been wet felted (pg. 22) slightly larger than the wire wings. **(Fig. 5)**

15. Wrap the edge of the felt sheet over the wire frame and felt into place with a regular felting needle. **(Fig. 6)** The center of the wing will be thinner than the outer edges and slightly transparent. This gives the wings an interesting look.

16. Attach wings on the back. Cut the doll's back and insert the center of wings. Add a small piece of wool batt and needle felt in place to hide the wires. **(Fig. 7)**

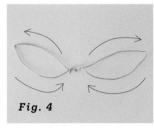

Fig. 4

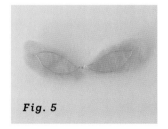

Fig. 5

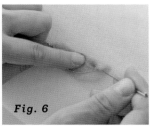

Fig. 6

Finishing

17. If desired, add decorative miniature roses to the head.

18. To pose the doll as shown on page 2, tilt the head slightly to the right. Bend the fingers around miniature flowers as if grasping the bouquet. Add movement to the wings by bending them at the tips slightly. Position the feet together, in line with the center of the body.

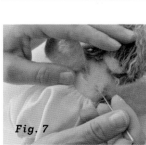

Fig. 7

Mermaid

Found lounging in blue lagoons and swimming in the sea with dolphins, this magical mermaid is a joy to make. Her tail is made of colorful felted fish scales that are smaller at the bottom and gradually grow in size.

Finished Size

- 5 in (12 cm) seated

Fibers

- **Head,** 7.5 g natural wool batt
- **Body,** 23 g natural wool batt
- **Eyes,** 1 g each of black, brown, and natural tone roving
- **Mouth,** 1 g each of peach and rose roving
- **Cheeks,** 1 g each peach and persimmon roving, blended
- **Scales,** three shades of felket or felt sheet about 6 x 6 in (15 x 15 cm) total, light blue, light gray, pale green shown

Wires

- **Body Core,** about 30 in (75 cm) of 8-gauge wire and about 6½ in (17 cm) of 12-gauge wire
- **Finger Core,** about 19¾ in (50 cm) of 28-gauge wire

Yarns

- **Body Base,** Sonomono Alpaca Wool; worsted weight, natural colorway (or other worsted-weight alpaca yarn)
- **Fingers,** Sonomono DK; DK weight, natural colorway (or other DK-weight wool yarn)
- **Hair,** plied fingering or worsted-weight tweed yarn in brown tones, cut to desired lengths and untwisted

Other

- **Wire crown,** 28-gauge copper wire and small shells

Tools

- Felting needles
- Sewing needle
- Chain nose pliers
- Scissors
- Stiletto
- Awl

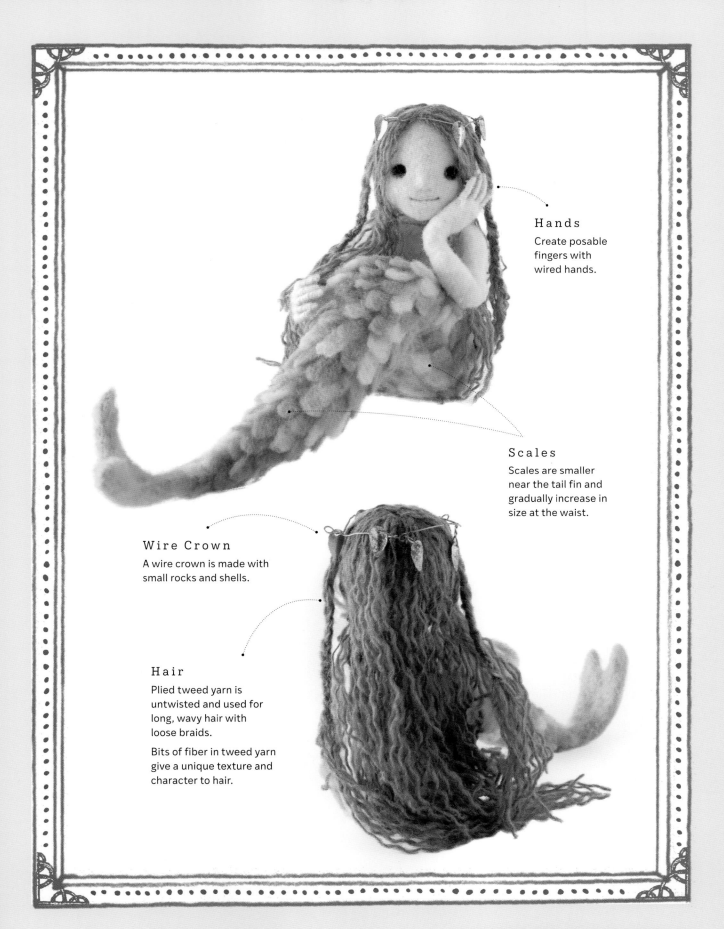

Hands
Create posable fingers with wired hands.

Scales
Scales are smaller near the tail fin and gradually increase in size at the waist.

Wire Crown
A wire crown is made with small rocks and shells.

Hair
Plied tweed yarn is untwisted and used for long, wavy hair with loose braids.

Bits of fiber in tweed yarn give a unique texture and character to hair.

Instructions

◆ ◆

Make the Doll

Referring to the step-by-step instructions in *Making a Felted Doll* (pgs. 26-47), create the Mermaid as follows:

Mermaid Head

1. Make the head with natural color wool batt before embellishing the face. Add eyes using black and brown roving for the eyeball color. Add rosy cheeks with peach and persimmon colored roving blended together. Add the mouth with peach and rose fiber.

2. Add hair to the head. Untwist brown tweed fingering or worsted-weight yarn. Needle felt the yarn to the head and trim to varying lengths. Add a simple, loose braid to each side of the head.

Mermaid Body

Note: The technique for constructing the Mermaid's body is fundamentally the same as a doll with legs. However, rather than forming individual legs, wires will be wrapped together to form the tail.

3. Make the body using 8-gauge wire for the core of the body. Cross the ends of the leg wires and twist to form the tail. Use 12-gauge wire for the arms. **(Fig. 1)**

4. Wrap the core of the body with wool batt. Secure the wool batt by wrapping worsted-weight alpaca yarn around the batt **(Fig. 2)**. Then, needle felt wool batt on top of the yarn to form the body. Leave the tail fin wires bare.

5. Once the body is formed, sculpt the arms by needle felting wool batt to the wrapped core wires. Use the technique on page 44 to create hands with posable fingers.

6. Attach the head to the body.

Mermaid Tail

7. Using blue felket or felt sheet that has been wet felted (pg. 22), cut a triangular piece for the tail fin slightly larger than the wire frame. **(Fig. 3)**

8. Wrap one edge of the felt sheet around one tail fin wire. Needle felt the felt sheet in place. **(Fig. 4)** Repeat for the other half of the tail fin.

9. Where the wool sheet overlaps in the center of the tail fin, needle felt the fibers and finalize the shape of the fin. **(Fig. 5)**

10. Using three shades of felket or felt sheet that have been wet felted, cut several small ovals for scales. **(Fig. 6)**

11. Working from the tail fin toward the waist, needle felt the scales to the tail in rows. Each new row should overlap the previous row slightly. **(Fig. 7)**

12. As you continue up the tail, gradually increase the size of the scales. Add scales until the entire tail is covered.

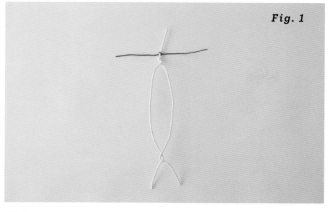

Fig. 1

Fig. 2

Fig. 3

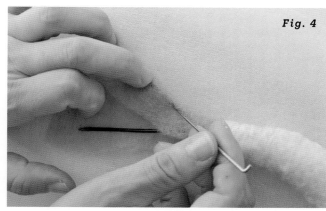

Fig. 4

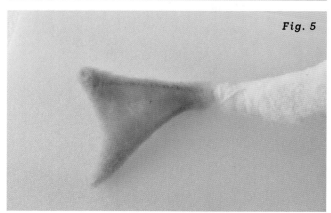

Fig. 5

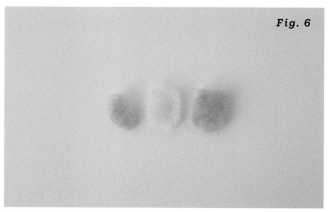

Fig. 6

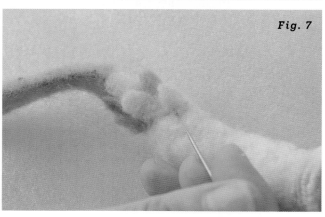

Fig. 7

Finishing

13. Make a miniature crown with copper wire and small stones or shells.

14. To pose the doll as shown on page 4, bend the tail so the mermaid is in a seated position. Twist the tail fin to curl upward slightly. Bend the left arm at the elbow and position the head to rest in the hand. Place the right hand on the tail as if holding at the knee.

Red Riding Hood

This sweet little girl is all dressed up in red to take a basket of goodies to her grandmother, or so the story goes. Along the way she meets a tricky wolf who would like her treats for himself.

Finished Size

- 6¼ in (16 cm) tall

Fibers

- **Head,** 5.5 g natural wool batt
- **Body,** 13 g natural wool batt
- **Eyes,** 1 g each of dark teal, slate blue, and natural tone roving
- **Mouth,** 1 g each of peach and rose roving
- **Cheeks,** 1 g each of pink and persimmon roving, blended
- **Hood,** red felket or felted sheet about 6½ x 6½ in (17 x 17 cm)
- **Apple,** 1 g red roving
- **Bread,** 1 g each of brown and dark brown roving

Wires

- **Body Core,** about 14¼ in (36 cm) of 8-gauge wire and about 6 in (15 cm) of 12-gauge wire

Yarns

- **Body Base,** Sonomono Alpaca Wool; worsted weight, natural colorway (or other worsted-weight alpaca yarn)
- **Fingers,** Sonomono DK; DK weight, natural colorway (or other DK-weight wool yarn)
- **Hair,** plied fingering or worsted-weight wool yarn in soft yellow

Fabrics

- **Dress,** red wool about 8 x 12 in (20 x 30 cm)
- **Apron,** white linen about 2¾ x 4¾ in (7 x 12 cm)
- **Shoes,** 1.5 mm thick leather about 2 x 6 in (5 x 15 cm) and black felt sheet about 1½ x 1¼ in (4 x 3 cm)
- **Basket,** 1.5 mm thick leather about 2¾ x 6 in (7 x 15 cm)

Other

- **Ribbon,** red 5 mm wide about 5 in (12 cm)
- **Ribbon,** black 3 mm wide about 12 in (30 cm)
- **Ribbon,** white 2 mm wide about 12 in (30 cm)
- Sewing thread

Tools

- Felting needles
- Sewing needle
- Chain nose pliers
- Scissors
- Stiletto
- Awl

Hair
Plied yellow yarn is untwisted for hair that is styled in a chignon.

Hands
Make a basic hand, without a wire core in the fingers.

Boots
Tall leather boots are stitched from the toe to the knee.

Basket
Red Riding Hood carries a basket of goodies.

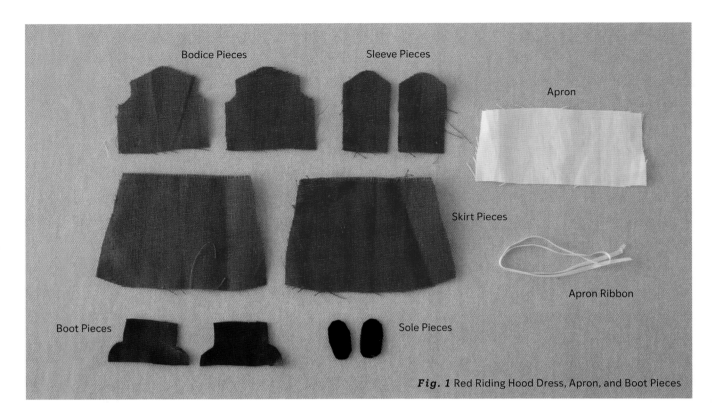

Fig. 1 Red Riding Hood Dress, Apron, and Boot Pieces

Bodice Pieces

Sleeve Pieces

Apron

Skirt Pieces

Apron Ribbon

Boot Pieces

Sole Pieces

Instructions

Make the Doll

Referring to the step-by-step instructions in *Making a Felted Doll* (pgs. 26-47), create Red Riding Hood as follows:

1.   Make the head with natural color wool batt before embellishing the face. Add eyes using natural color roving in the eye socket, with dark teal and slate blue for the eyeball color. Add rosy cheeks with pink and persimmon colored roving blended together. Add the mouth with peach and rose fiber.

2.   Add hair to the head. Untwist yellow fingering or worsted-weight plied yarn. Needle felt the yarn to the head following the Chignon instructions on pg. 37. Tie a red ribbon bow around the bun.

3.   Make the body using 8-gauge wire for the core of the body and legs and 12-gauge wire for the arms. The core wires are wrapped in worsted weight alpaca wool yarn and then natural color wool batt is needle felted to the core.

4.   Once the body is formed, sculpt the arms and legs by needle felting wool batt to the wrapped core wires. Make the hands using the basic hand instructions (pg. 43).

5.   Temporarily attach the head to the body.

Sew the Clothes

Referring to *Sewing Clothes & Shoes* (pgs. 48-51) as needed, make Red Riding Hood's dress, apron, cape, and shoes as follows:

Dress

6. Using the photo shown **(Fig. 1)**, cut the dress pieces from red wool fabric.

Note: Each doll is unique based on the amount of wool batt used to make the body. As a result, pattern pieces cannot be standardized. Pieces should be cut to fit your doll.

7. Align the front and back bodice pieces with right sides together. Sew the shoulder and side seams. Turn right side out.

8. Remove the doll's head. Put the bodice on the body. Attach the sleeves. Reattach the head. The head fully covers the neckline of the dress, so the neckline does not require finishing.

9. Align the skirt pieces with right sides together. Sew together along the sides. Turn the skirt right side out.

10. Gather the skirt waist and sew it to the dress bodice. You may find it easiest to sew the skirt directly to the doll's body when attaching to the bodice.

11. To hem the skirt, fold a scant amount of the bottom of the skirt to the wrong side and sew.

Apron

12. Hem the two short sides and one long side of a piece of white linen. Gather the fourth side with running stitch. Sew white ribbon along the gathered edge. **(Fig. 2)**

13. Wrap the apron around the waist of the doll and tie the ends of the ribbon in a bow in the back.

Fig. 2

Fig. 3

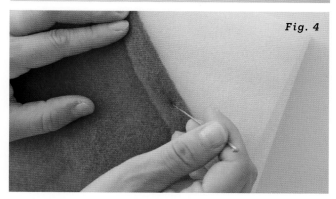
Fig. 4

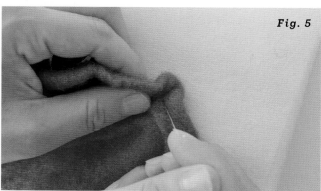
Fig. 5

Fig. 6

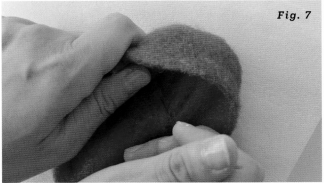

Fig. 7

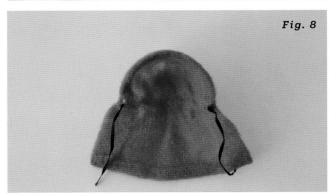

Fig. 8

Hood

Note: The reference images for these steps begin on the previous page.

14. Trim the top corners off a square piece of red felket or felt sheet that has been wet felted. **(Fig. 3)**

15. Fold the bottom edge over ⅜ in (1 cm) and needle felt in place. Fold the top edge and trimmed corners over ⅜ in (1 cm) and needle felt in place, creating a channel for the ribbon. **(Fig. 4)**

16. Gather the fiber and shape into the hood. **(Fig. 5)**

17. Try the hood on the doll and adjust the shape as needed. **(Fig. 6)**

18. Gather the back neck of the hood to separate the hood from the cape. Needle felt the gathered fabric. **(Fig. 7)**

19. Thread black ribbon through the channel made in Step 15. **(Fig. 8)** Place the hood on the doll and tie the ribbon in a bow.

Shoes

20. Cut two pieces of leather for the boots and two soles using the image on page 74 as a guide. **(Fig. 1)**

21. Wrap one boot piece around the foot of the doll and stitch from toe to knee. Repeat for the second shoe.

22. Glue the soles to the bottoms of the feet and trim excess.

Finishing

23. Make a leather basket (pg. 61), an apple (pg. 59), and a loaf of bread (pg. 59).

24. To pose the doll as shown on page 6, tilt the head as if to look away from the wolf.

The Wolf

Tall and lean, this wolf is hungry for the treats that Red Riding Hood is taking to her grandmother. To make him, you'll combine doll making and personifying techniques.

Finished Size

- 8 ¼ in (21 cm) tall

Fibers

- **Head,** 8.5 g natural wool batt
- **Body,** 17 g natural wool batt
- **Fur,** 1 g each of brown, natural tone, light gray, and dark gray roving, blended
- **Eyes,** 1 g each of dark teal, blue, and natural tone roving
- **Nose & Mouth,** 1 g dark brown roving
- **Ears,** natural tone and brown felket or felt sheet about 4 x 2½ in (10 x 5 cm)

Wires

- **Body Core,** about 19½ in (50 cm) of 8-gauge wire and about 8 in (20 cm) of 12-gauge wire
- **Finger Core,** about 19½ in (50 cm) of 28-gauge wire

Yarns

- **Body Base,** Sonomono Alpaca Wool; worsted weight, natural colorway (or other worsted-weight alpaca yarn)
- **Fingers,** DK-weight tweed yarn, brown colorway

Fabrics

- **Shirt,** white linen about 8 x 4 in (20 x 10 cm)
- **Pants,** gray wool about 6 x 6 in (15 x 15 cm)
- **Suspenders,** 3 mm leather cord about 14 in (36 cm)
- **Shoes,** 1.5 mm thick leather about 2 x 6 in (5 x 15 cm) and black felt sheet about 1½ x 1¼ in (4 x 3 cm)

Other

- **Buttons,** four 5 mm diameter
- One miniature flower (optional)
- Sewing thread

Tools

- Felting needles
- Sewing needle
- Chain nose pliers
- Scissors
- Stiletto
- Awl

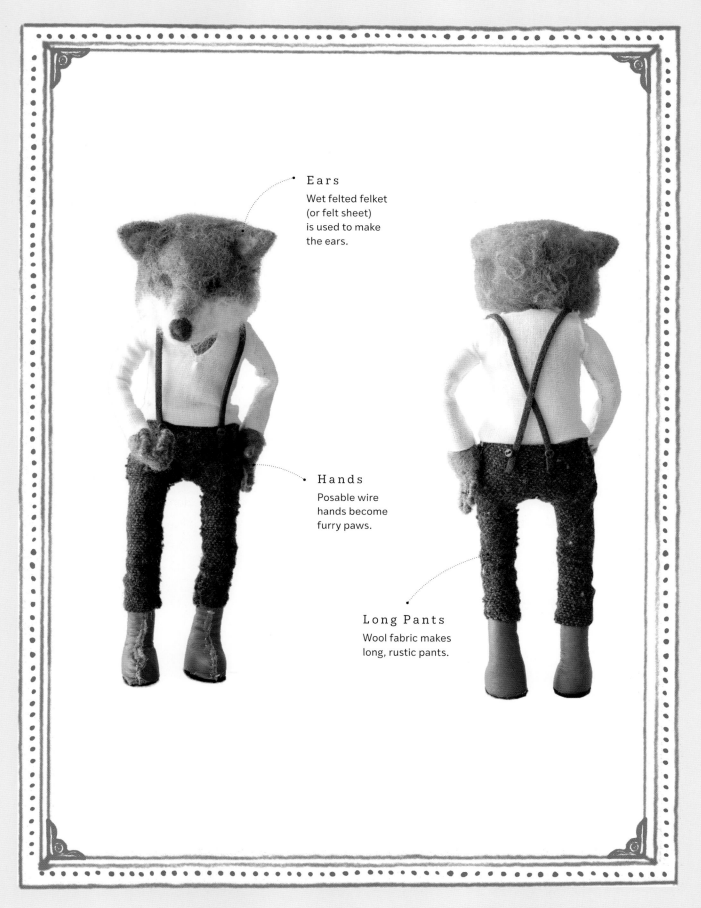

Ears
Wet felted felket
(or felt sheet)
is used to make
the ears.

Hands
Posable wire
hands become
furry paws.

Long Pants
Wool fabric makes
long, rustic pants.

Instructions

❖❖

Make the Doll

Referring to the step-by-step instructions in *Making a Felted Doll, Part 5: Personifying an Animal* (pgs. 52-55), create The Wolf as follows:

1. Make the head with natural color wool batt before embellishing the face. The head should be egg-shaped with an elongated snout. Add the mouth and nose using brown wool roving. **(Fig. 1 and 2)**

2. Lightly blend brown, natural tone, light gray, and dark gray roving to create the fur. Layer the blended roving on the head and down the top of the snout, leaving the mouth and lower face natural.

3. Add eyes using natural color roving in the eye socket, with blue and dark teal for the eyeball color.

4. Wet felt (pg. 22) brown felket or felt sheet and cut into small triangles for the ears. Repeat with natural tone felket or felt sheet, making the triangles slightly smaller than the brown ones. Layer the inner ear piece on top of the outer ear piece and needle felt together. Add the ears to the head.

5. Make the body using 8-gauge wire for the core of the body and legs and 12-gauge wire for the arms. The core wires are wrapped in worsted-weight alpaca wool yarn and then natural color wool batt is needle felted to the core. Do not add too much batt to the doll to exaggerate his lean look.

Fig. 1

6. Once the body is formed, sculpt the arms and legs by needle felting wool batt to the wrapped core wires. Make posable hands (pg. 44), slightly oversized and wrapped in tweed yarn. Attach the hands to the arms.

7. Temporarily attach the head to the body.

Fig. 2

Sew the Clothes

Referencing *Sewing Clothes & Shoes* (pgs. 48-51) as needed, make The Wolf's clothes as follows:

Clothing

8. Using white linen, cut a shirt front, shirt back, and two sleeves. Use the image of bodice pieces shown in Fig. 1 on page 67 as a guide, but make the following modifications. First, for the front bodice piece, cut a v-neck instead of a rounded neckline. Second, for the back bodice piece, do not cut the notch for the wings. This fabric does not have stretch, so it will be sewn directly to the doll's body.

Note: Each doll is unique based on the amount of wool batt used to make the body. As a result, pattern pieces cannot be standardized. Pieces should be cut to fit your doll.

9. Align the front and back shirt pieces with right sides together. Sew the shoulder seams together. Turn right side out.

10. Make a few cuts along the V of the neckline, fold the edge to the wrong side, and stitch in place.

11. Remove the head of the doll. Put the shirt on the body, sew the side seams together, and attach the sleeves. Reattach the head.

12. Using wool fabric, cut a pant front and a pant back similar to that shown in Step 11 of *Pants & Shorts* (pg. 50), but with a longer inseam. With right sides together, sew just the outside seams. Do not sew the inseam. Turn right side out.

13. Slide the pants onto the doll's body. Stitch the inseam directly to the legs. Fold the waist edge to the wrong side and stitch in place.

14. Cut the 14 in (36 cm) length of leather cord in half to make two suspenders. Stitch each end of the suspender in place at the top of the pant, crossing the cords in the back. Sew a button in place on top of the leather cord each place where it attaches to the pants.

Shoes

15. Cut two pieces of leather for the boots and two pieces of felt for the soles.

16. Wrap one boot piece around the foot of the doll and stitch from toe to ankle. Repeat for the second shoe.

17. Glue the soles to the bottoms of the feet and trim excess.

Finishing

18. To pose the doll as shown on page 6, form the posable hand to hold a miniature flower. Extend the arm so that it appears it is offering the flower to Red Riding Hood. Tilt the head down and slightly hunch the body so it looms over Red Riding Hood and creates an imposing impression.

Reading Friends, Boy

Get carried away with your imagination when making the first of two friends who love to read together. Posable fingers help the boy hold his beloved books.

Finished Size

- 6¼ in (15.5 cm) tall

Fibers

- **Head,** 6.5 g natural wool batt
- **Body,** 13 g natural wool batt
- **Eyes,** 1 g each of natural tone, brown, and charcoal roving
- **Mouth,** 1 g each of peach and rose roving
- **Cheeks,** 1 g each of pink and persimmon roving, blended

Wires

- **Body Core,** about 14¼ in (36 cm) of 8-gauge wire and about 6 in (15 cm) of 12-gauge wire
- **Finger Core,** about 19¾ in (50 cm) of 28-gauge wire
- **Glasses,** about 12 in (30 cm) of 24-gauge wire

Yarns

- **Body Base,** Sonomono Alpaca Wool; worsted weight, natural colorway (or other worsted-weight alpaca yarn)

- **Fingers,** Sonomono DK; DK weight, natural colorway (or other DK-weight wool yarn)
- **Hair,** Sonomono Alpaca Wool; worsted weight, gray colorway (or other worsted-weight alpaca yarn)

Fabrics

- **Shirt,** brown linen about 8 x 4 in (20 x 10 cm)
- **Shorts,** patterned wool about 6 x 4 in (15 x 10 cm)
- **Shoes,** synthetic suede about 6 x 2 in (15 x 5 cm) and black felt sheet about 1½ x 1¼ in (4 x 3 cm)
- **Book,** 2 mm leather about 3 x 1¼ in (7.5 x 3 cm) and white linen, 3-4 pieces slightly smaller than the leather piece

Other

- Sewing thread

Tools

- Felting needles
- Sewing needle
- Chain nose pliers
- Scissors
- Stiletto
- Awl

Hair
Untwisted alpaca yarn is used in a short hairstyle.

Hands
Posable wire hands allow this doll to hold objects like books.

Boots
Synthetic suede fabric is used to make soft, hand stitched shoes.

Instructions

Make the Doll

Referring to the step-by-step instructions in *Making a Felted Doll* (pgs. 26-47), create the boy as follows:

1. Make the head with natural color wool batt before embellishing the face. Add eyes using natural color roving in the eye socket, with brown and charcoal for the eyeball color. Add rosy cheeks with pink and persimmon colored roving blended together. Add the mouth with peach and rose fiber.

2. Add hair to the head. Untwist gray worsted-weight plied yarn. Needle felt the yarn to the head following the Short Hair instructions on page 39.

3. Make the body using 8-gauge wire for the core of the body and legs and 12-gauge wire for the arms. The core wires are wrapped in worsted-weight alpaca wool yarn and then natural color wool batt is needle felted to the core.

4. Once the body is formed, sculpt the arms and legs by needle felting wool batt to the wrapped core wires. Make the hands using the posable hand instructions (pg. 44). Attach the hands to the arms.

5. Temporarily attach the head to the body.

Sew the Clothes

Referring to *Sewing Clothes & Shoes* (pgs. 48-51) as needed, make the boy's shirt, shorts, and shoes as follows:

Clothing

6. Using the bodice and sleeve pieces of *Cindy's Dress* (pg. 97, Fig. 1) as a guide, cut a shirt front, shirt back, and two sleeves.

Note: Each doll is unique based on the amount of wool batt used to make the body. As a result, pattern pieces cannot be standardized. Pieces should be cut to fit your doll.

7. Align the front and back shirt pieces with right sides together. Sew the shoulder seams together. Turn right side out.

8. Remove the head of the doll. Put the shirt on the body, sew the side seams together, and attach the sleeves. Reattach the head. The head fully covers the neckline of the shirt, so the neckline does not require finishing.

9. Using patterned wool fabric, cut a short front and a short back. With right sides together, sew the side seams and inseam. Turn right side out.

10. Fold the edge of the waist to the wrong side and stitch in place. Fold the edge of each leg of the shorts to the wrong side and stitch in place.

11. Put the shorts on the doll. Stitch the waist to the body, if needed.

Shoes

12. Using synthetic suede fabric, cut two boots. Cut two soles from felt sheet.

13. Wrap one boot piece around the foot of the doll and stitch from toe to knee. Repeat for the second shoe.

14. Glue the soles to the bottoms of the feet and trim excess.

Make the Accessories

15. Using the instructions on page 60, make wire glasses and a book. Place the wire glasses on the boy and hook the temples over the ears.

Finishing

16. To pose the doll as shown, balance in a standing position with the knees slightly bent, and arrange the hands to hold an open book. Tilt the head down as if reading.

Reading Friends, Rabbit

The studious and furry partner of the Reading Friends, the rabbit is a personified animal with a lot of character. Make him just as tall as the boy to enhance his charm.

Finished Size

- 6½ in (16.5 cm) tall, to the ears

Fibers

- **Head,** 6 g natural wool batt
- **Body,** 11.5 g natural wool batt
- **Fur,** 2 g gray roving
- **Eyes,** 1 g each of natural tone, dark teal, and blue roving
- **Mouth & Nose,** 1 g light brown roving
- **Cheeks,** 1 g pink roving
- **Ears,** natural tone and light gray felket or felt sheet about 4 x 4 in (10 x 10 cm)

Wires

- **Body Core,** about 14¼ in (36 cm) of 8-gauge wire and about 6 in (15 cm) of 12-gauge wire
- **Glasses,** about 12 in (30 cm) of 24-gauge wire

Yarns

- **Body Base,** Sonomono Alpaca Wool; worsted weight, natural colorway (or other worsted-weight alpaca yarn)
- **Fingers,** Sonomono DK; DK weight, natural colorway (or other DK-weight wool yarn)

Fabrics

- **Shorts,** gray wool about 6 x 4 in (15 x 10 cm)
- **Shoes,** 1.5 mm thick leather about 2 x 6 in (5 x 15 cm) and black felt sheet about 1½ x 1¼ in (4 x 3 cm)
- **Suspenders,** 3 mm leather cord about 12 in (30 cm)
- **Book,** 2 mm leather about 3 x 1¼ in (7.5 x 3 cm) and white linen, 3-4 pieces slightly smaller than the leather piece

Other

- **Buttons,** four 5 mm diameter
- Sewing thread

Tools

- Felting needles
- Sewing needle
- Chain nose pliers
- Scissors
- Stiletto
- Awl

Ears

Wet felted felket or felt sheet create tall ears with structure.

Hands

Needle felt a basic "mitten hand" for paws.

Legs

Make the rabbit's body slightly longer and the legs slightly shorter than the boy's to balance their appearances.

Instructions

❖ ❖

Make the Doll

Detailed step-by-step instructions for Reading Friends, Rabbit are shown in *Making a Felted Doll, Part 5: Personifying an Animal* (pgs. 52-55).

1. Make the head with natural color wool batt before adding gray roving for fur. Add eyes using natural color roving in the eye sockets, with dark teal and blue for the eyeballs. Add rosy cheeks with pink roving. Add the mouth and nose with light brown fiber.

2. Wet felt (pg. 22) gray and natural tone felket or felt sheet to make the ears. Attach the ears to the head.

3. Make the body using 8-gauge wire for the core of the body and legs, and use 12-gauge wire for the arms. The core wires are wrapped in worsted-weight alpaca wool yarn and then gray colored wool roving is felted to the core.

4. Once the body is formed, sculpt the arms and legs by needle felting roving to the wrapped core wires. Make basic hands and attach them to the arms.

5. Attach the head to the body.

Sew the Clothes

Referring to *Sewing Clothes & Shoes* (pgs. 48-51) as needed, make the rabbit's shorts and shoes as follows:

Clothing

6. Using the photo shown **(Fig. 1)**, cut the shorts from a piece of gray wool fabric. With right sides together, sew the side seam and inseam. Turn right side out.

Note: Each doll is unique based on the amount of wool batt used to make the body. As a result, pattern pieces cannot be standardized. Pieces should be cut to fit your doll.

7. Fold the edge of the waist to the wrong side and stitch in place. Fold the edge of each leg of the shorts to the wrong side and stitch in place. **(Fig. 2)**

8. Put the shorts on the doll. **(Fig. 3)** Stitch the waist to the body. **(Fig. 4)**

9. Cut the 12 in (30 cm) length of leather cord in half to make two suspenders. Stitch each end of the suspender in place at the top of the pant **(Fig. 5)**, crossing the cords in the back **(Fig. 6)**. Sew a button in place on top of the leather cord each place where it attaches to the pants **(Fig. 7)**.

Shoes

10. Using the photo shown **(Fig. 1)**, cut two boots from leather and two soles from black felt sheet.

11. Wrap one boot piece around the foot of the doll **(Fig. 8)** and stitch from toe to knee **(Fig. 9)**. Repeat for the second shoe.

12. Glue the soles to the bottoms of the feet **(Fig. 10)** and trim excess.

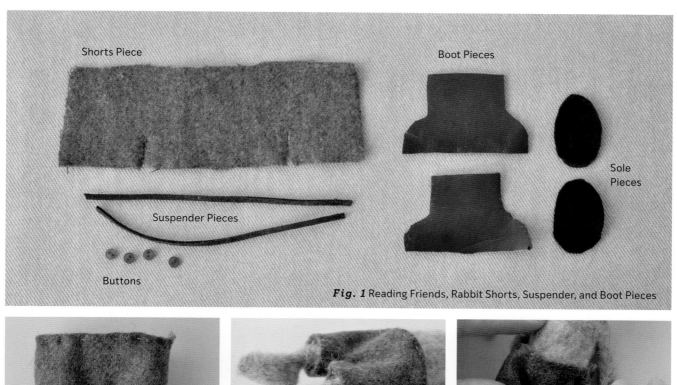

Shorts Piece

Boot Pieces

Suspender Pieces

Sole Pieces

Buttons

Fig. 1 Reading Friends, Rabbit Shorts, Suspender, and Boot Pieces

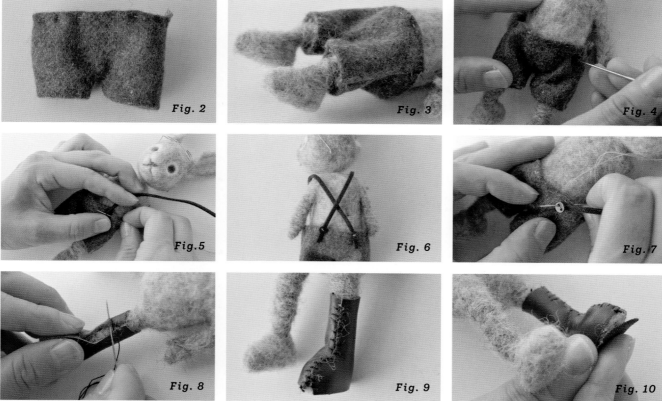

Fig. 2

Fig. 3

Fig. 4

Fig.5

Fig. 6

Fig. 7

Fig. 8

Fig. 9

Fig. 10

Make the Accessories

13. Using the instructions on page 60, make wire glasses and a book. Place the wire glasses on the rabbit above the eyes, as if resting on the forehead.

Finishing

14. To pose the doll as shown on page 8, balance in a standing position with the knees slightly bent and belly pushed forward. Tuck the book between the arm and the body.

Librarian

Bundled up for winter, the librarian walks through snow to her shelves of books. To create an older doll, the legs and arms are longer, and the head is smaller compared to the body.

Finished Size

- 7¾ in (20 cm) tall

Fibers

- **Head,** 7 g natural wool batt
- **Body,** 15 g natural wool batt
- **Eyes,** 1 g each of natural tone, brown, and charcoal roving
- **Mouth,** 1 g each of peach and rose roving
- **Cheeks,** 1 g each of pink and persimmon roving, blended
- **Tights,** light gray felket or felt sheet about 4 x 4 in (10 x 10 cm)
- **Hat,** white felket or felt sheet about 3 x 3 in (7.5 x 7.5 cm)

Wires

- **Body Core,** about 15 in (38 cm) of 8-gauge wire and about 6 in (15 cm) of 12-gauge wire
- **Finger Core,** about 19¾ in (50 cm) of 28-gauge wire

Yarns

- **Body Base,** Sonomono Alpaca Wool; worsted weight, natural colorway (or other worsted-weight alpaca yarn)
- **Fingers,** Sonomono DK; DK weight, natural colorway (or other DK-weight wool yarn)
- **Hair,** fingering-weight yarn, yellow colorway
- **Scarf,** scrap white wool yarn, any weight

Fabrics

- **Dress,** beige wool about 8 x 8 in (20 x 20 cm)
- **Scarf,** white wool about 8 x ⅝ in (20 x 1.5 cm)
- **Shoes,** leather about 6 x 4 in (15 x 10 cm) and black felt sheet about 1½ x 1¼ in (4 x 3 cm)
- **Bag,** 2 mm leather about 4 x 4 in (10 x 10 cm)

Other

- Sewing thread

Tools

- Felting needles
- Sewing needle
- Chain nose pliers
- Scissors
- Stiletto
- Awl

Hair
Untwisted plied fingering-weight yarn is used in a short, one-length hairstyle.

Hat
Hand knit a hat (pg. 56) or use white felket or felt sheet to make a cozy hat.

Scarf
Cut wool fabric into a long scarf and needle felt scrap wool yarn for fringe for a quick and easy accessory.

Instructions

Make the Doll

Referring to the step-by-step instructions in *Making a Felted Doll* (pgs. 26-47), create the Librarian as follows:

1. Make the head with natural color wool batt before embellishing the face. Add eyes using natural color roving in the eye socket, with brown and black for the eyeball color. Add rosy cheeks with pink and persimmon colored roving blended together. Add the mouth with peach and rose fiber.

2. Add hair to the head. Untwist yellow fingering-weight plied yarn. Needle felt the yarn to the head following the Short Hairstyle instructions on page 39.

3. Make the body using 8-gauge wire for the core of the body and legs and 12-gauge wire for the arms. The core wires are wrapped in worsted-weight alpaca wool yarn and then natural color wool batt is needle felted to the core.

4. Once the body is formed, sculpt the arms by needle felting wool batt to the wrapped core wires. For the legs, needle felt light gray felket or felt sheet as if the doll is wearing tights. Make the hands using the posable hand instructions (pg. 44) and attach to the arms.

5. Temporarily attach the head to the body.

Sew the Clothes

Referring to *Sewing Clothes & Shoes* (pgs. 48-51) as needed, make the librarian's dress and shoes as follows:

Dress

6. Using the photo shown **(Fig. 1)**, cut the dress pieces from beige wool fabric.

Note: Each doll is unique based on the amount of wool batt used to make the body. As a result, pattern pieces cannot be standardized. Pieces should be cut to fit your doll.

7. Align the front and back dress pieces with right sides together. Sew the shoulder and side seams. Turn right side out.

8. Remove the doll's head. Put the dress on the body. Attach the sleeves. Reattach the head. The head fully covers the neckline of the dress, so the neckline does not require finishing.

9. To create the fringe at the bottom of the dress, pull out 3-4 threads of the fabric to fray the edge. **(Fig. 2)** No other finishing to the edge is required.

Shoes

10. Cut two pieces of leather for the boots and two soles from black felt sheet using the image as a guide. **(Fig. 1)**

11. Wrap one boot piece around the foot of the doll and stitch from toe to knee. Repeat for the second shoe.

12. Glue the soles to the bottoms of the feet and trim excess.

Make the Accessories

Hat

Note: There are several ways to make a doll hat. To knit a hat, follow the instructions on page 56. The instructions that follow here use felket or felt sheet. Needle felting the hat to the head is optional.

13. Wet felt a piece of felket or felt sheet. Once dry, wrap the felt sheet around the doll's head to get an approximate circumference of the hat. Using the hat schematic **(Fig. 3)** as a general guide, cut a rectangle of felt with 3 triangles of material removed.

14. Bring the short ends of the felt hat piece together and needle felt the edges together. Adjust the triangle pieces toward the crown of the hat and needle felt in place. **(Fig. 4)** Turn the hat right side out and attach to the head.

Scarf

Note: Like the hat, there are several ways to make a doll scarf. To knit a scarf, follow the instructions on page 57. You can also use felket or felt sheet. The instructions that follow here use wool fabric.

15. Cut a long, narrow strip of white wool fabric to 8 in (20 cm) long and ⅝ in (1.5 cm) wide. Needle felt scrap yarn to the short ends of the wool fabric to act as fringe.

Bag

16. Using the photo as a guide **(Fig. 5)**, cut the bag pieces from leather fabric.

17. Sew the short side of the large bag piece wrong sides together. Sew the bottom of the bag to the piece just seamed. Sew the ends of the handles to the body of the bag.

Finishing

18. Every librarian needs a book! Using the instructions on page 60, make a book.

19. To pose the doll as shown on page 10, position the doll standing upright with a straight back, move the posable fingers to hold the book. Tilt the head down as if the doll is reading the book.

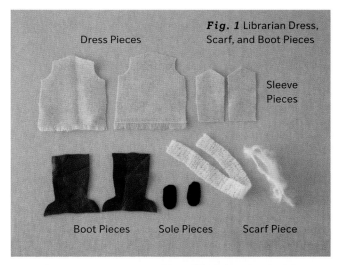

Fig. 1 Librarian Dress, Scarf, and Boot Pieces

Dress Pieces

Sleeve Pieces

Boot Pieces   Sole Pieces   Scarf Piece

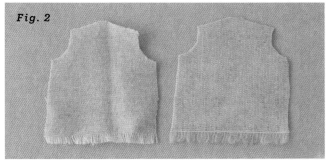

Fig. 2

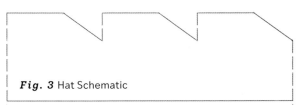

Fig. 3 Hat Schematic

Fig. 4

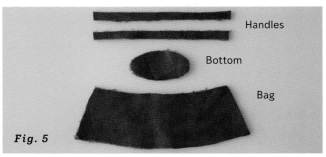

Fig. 5

Handles

Bottom

Bag

Cindy & Her Teddy Bear

The simplicity of this doll draws extra attention to her features. With that in mind, take care and play up the sweetness in the details of her face.

Finished Size

- 7 in (18 cm) tall

Fibers

- **Head,** 6.5 g natural wool batt
- **Body,** 16 g natural wool batt
- **Eyes,** 1 g each of dark teal, slate blue, and natural tone roving
- **Mouth,** 1 g each of peach and rose roving
- **Cheeks,** 1 g each of pink and persimmon roving, blended
- **Teddy Bear,** 5 g gray wool batt or roving

Wires

- **Body Core,** about 14¼ in (36 cm) of 8-gauge wire and about 6 in (15 cm) of 12-gauge wire

Yarns

- **Body Base,** Sonomono Alpaca Wool; worsted weight, natural colorway (or other worsted-weight alpaca yarn)
- **Fingers,** Sonomono DK; DK weight, natural colorway (or other DK-weight wool yarn)
- **Hair,** plied fingering or worsted-weight wool yarn in light gray colorway

Fabrics

- **Dress,** brown wool about 8 x 12 in (20 x 30 cm)
- **Shorts,** white striped linen about 6 x 6 in (15 x 15 cm)
- **Shoes,** brown felt sheet about 6 x 6 in (15 x 15 cm) and black felt sheet about 1½ x 1¼ in (4 x 3 cm)

Others

- **Ribbon,** green 5 mm wide about 10 in (25 cm)
- **Embroidery Floss,** one skein of lavender
- **Buttons,** two 5 mm diameter
- Sewing thread

Tools

- Felting needles
- Sewing needle
- Chain nose pliers
- Scissors
- Stiletto
- Awl

Bows
Tie ribbon into bows and sew to the head for a sweet, youthful look.

Buttons
Small 5 mm buttons act as eyes on this doll's favorite teddy bear.

Instructions

❖ ◆ ❖

Make the Doll

Detailed step-by-step instructions for Cindy are shown in *Making a Felted Doll, Parts 1-3 (pgs. 26-47).*

1. Make the head with natural color wool batt before embellishing the face. Add eyes using natural color roving in the eye socket, with dark teal and slate blue for the eyeball color. Add rosy cheeks with pink and persimmon colored roving blended together. Add the mouth with peach and rose fiber.

2. Add hair to the head. Untwist gray fingering-weight plied yarn. Needle felt the yarn to the head following the Short Hair instructions on page 39. Tie green ribbon into small bows and attach to each side of the head.

3. Make the body using 8-gauge wire for the core of the body and legs and 12-gauge wire for the arms. The core wires are wrapped in worsted-weight alpaca wool yarn and then natural color wool batt is needle felted to the core.

4. Once the body is formed, sculpt the arms and legs by needle felting wool batt to the wrapped core wires. Make the hands using the basic hand instructions (pg. 43).

5. Temporarily attach the head to the body.

Sew the Clothes

Detailed step-by-step instructions for sewing Cindy's clothes are shown in *Making a Felted Doll, Part 4: Sewing Clothes & Shoes (pgs. 48-51).*

Dress

6. Using the photo shown **(Fig. 1)**, cut the dress pieces from brown wool fabric.

Note: Each doll is unique based on the amount of wool batt used to make the body. As a result, pattern pieces cannot be standardized. Pieces should be cut to fit your doll.

7. Align the front and back bodice pieces with right sides together. Sew the shoulder and side seams. Turn right side out.

Shorts

12. Using the photo shown as a guide **(Fig. 1)**, cut the shorts pieces from striped linen fabric.

13. Align the shorts pieces with right sides together. Sew the side seams and inseam. **(Fig. 2)** Turn right side out.

8. Remove the doll's head. Put the bodice on the body. Attach the sleeves. Reattach the head. The head fully covers the neckline of the dress, so the neckline does not require finishing.

9. Align the skirt pieces with right sides together. Sew together along the sides. Turn the skirt right side out.

10. Gather the skirt waist and sew it to the dress bodice. You may find it easiest to sew the skirt directly to the doll's body when attaching to the bodice.

11. To hem the skirt, fold a scant amount of the bottom of the skirt to the wrong side and sew.

14. Fold the hem of each pant leg toward the wrong side and sew running stitch to gather. **(Fig. 3)** Do the same to gather the waist.

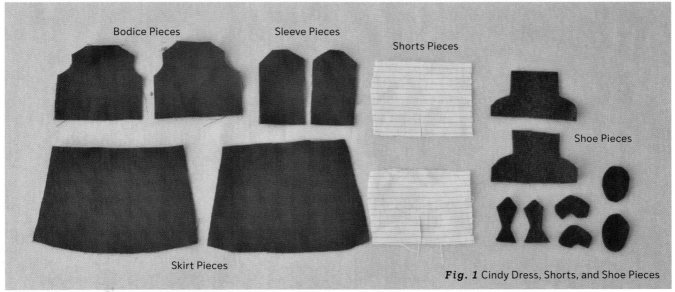

Bodice Pieces   Sleeve Pieces   Shorts Pieces   Shoe Pieces

Skirt Pieces

Fig. 1 Cindy Dress, Shorts, and Shoe Pieces

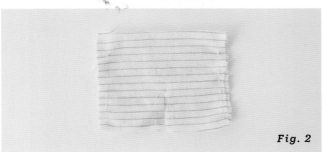

Fig. 2

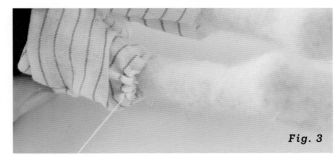

Fig. 3

Shoes

Detailed step-by-step instructions for sewing Cindy's shoes are shown in *Making a Felted Doll, Part 4: Sewing Clothes & Shoes (pgs. 48-51).*

15. Using the photo shown as a guide **(Fig. 1)**, cut two pieces of felt for the boots, two for the toes, two for the tongues, and two soles.

16. Position the tongue on the foot and ankle, then wrap one boot piece around the foot of the doll and stitch from toe to ankle. Repeat for the second shoe.

17. Glue the toe pieces to each shoe toe. Glue the soles to the bottoms of the feet and trim excess.

Make the Accessories

18. Following the instructions on page 58, make a teddy bear with gray wool batt or roving. Stitch buttons for eyes and add a ribbon around the neck.

Finishing

19. To pose the doll as shown on page 12, adjust to a standing position with the belly slightly forward. Tuck the teddy bear between the arm and body. Tilt the head slightly to one side.

Chapter Five

Inspirational Gallery

Once you've learned the basic techniques for making felt dolls, the variations you can do to make each consecutive doll unique are limited only by your imagination. What follows here is a gallery of dolls from my personal collection as well as those who use my methods. I hope they inspire you to adventure beyond what you've been shown and into the world of possibilities.

The Woodland Prince & His Fox

Boy & Bluebird

Harriet & Her Hare Cape

Warm Woolen Friends

Robert the Rabbit

The Musician

Jasmine

Artist: yukie ogawa

Artist Tip

The base is made with wool batt and wire. A mixture of solid white and natural blend beige is used for the skin color. To create the natural look of the face, I mixed wool colors and felted to create blended effects.

From the artist: I made this doll inspired by the heroine Jasmin from my favorite movie *Bagdad Cafe*.

Luna

Artist: misato

Artist Tip

The face and the body are made with wool batt. To create the tail, I used a mixture of iridescent sequins overtop of blended wools. I also added beaded bracelets to the wrist.

From the artist: I wanted to make a realistic doll using the soft texture of wool felt. This mermaid is young— she's just about to enter into adulthood.

Girl with a Bird

Artist: naco*(miminaco*lapin)

Artist Tip

To achieve this look, make a round face first, then add dots or lines at the position of eyes, nose, mouth, and cheeks. Add wool along the guidelines, such as the eyelid line. For the clothes, make a simple one-piece dress and line the edges with lace trim.

From the artist: I tried to make a character reminiscent of one you might see in a scene from a story. I incorporated a precious java sparrow in my project. I was inspired by the soft imagery of a watercolor painting and I hope you can feel that in my finished piece.

Bear Costumes

Artist: midori iro

Artist Tip

To more easily achieve the one-legged, dancing position, make the heel of the dolls very firm. Also, bigger heads make these dolls cuter. The heavier head needs to be sewn to the body. Be sure to take extra time to needle felt the seam smooth.

From the artist: I do not use glue in my projects to maintain the texture of the wool. To position these dancing bears, the legs and arms can be bent, and they can stand up by themselves.

Playing with Airplanes

Artist: midori iro

Artist Tip

To create this unique facial expression, align the eyes, ears, and nose on a very round head. Position rosy cheeks wide apart and below the eyes, nose, and mouth. The mouth is kept tight to the nose and forms a gentle grin.

From the artist: An oversized head and smaller body make these playful children very cute. Look for miniature accessories like these small airplanes for your dolls to play with.

Go Back to the Forest

Artist: rai * chi

Artist Tip

The body base is made with wire and wool batt, and natural blend roving is stabbed as the skin color. Stab small amounts of skin color wool as you adjust to make the face look three dimensional. The hands are made with five wired fingers. Wet felt wool felket into a sheet to make a skirt and combine it with a fabric blouse.

From the artist: Dolls have a tendency to look scary if they're too realistic, so I try to make my dolls cute. This is achieved by creating an oversized, cartoon-inspired head.

Takaramono (treasure)

Artist: Yukari

Artist Tip
Natural wool batt is used as a base for this doll, and everything else is made with wool roving. Chubby cheeks, rounded shoulders and back, and curling legs are unique to toddlers and are represented here.

From the artist: My baby was the model for this doll. I emphasized her chubby face and cute expression. Her smile always soothes everyone.

Let's Live Together

Artist: WOOLWOOL Tugane Kana

Artist Tip
Like many other artists, I think a larger head makes a doll feel cuter. So I did that with this young boy who is making friends with a musical bear.

From the artist: In Hokkaido, if a bear enters the city, he will be killed. I often wonder if there is any way we can live together peacefully. What if a human could be good friends with a bear? Just like this project . . .

Snow?

Artist: Nami Turuta

Artist Tip

There are several features that make this doll unique that you can try out on your own dolls. First, look for interesting platforms, like wood blocks, to display your dolls. Next, have fun choosing colored roving for posable hands to create the look of mittens or gloves.

From the artist: The boy is looking at the sky asking, "Is it starting to snow?" Sequins represent the snow and a single snowflake has landed in his hand, with others falling on his clothes.

Treasure

Artist: Inco

Artist Tip

The fluffiness of the rabbit suit is created by stabbing curls from curly wool locks. Sew felt together to make the hood before covering it in curly wool locks too.

From the artist: This boy is wearing his favorite rabbit suit. The sky blue and dandelion color balloons are his treasure.

Let's Go Soon!

Artist: Yoshiko Takinami

Artist Tip

I made the base of this doll using wool batt and added skin color using felket. The cheeks and lips are colored with light pink. The wide forehead and plump cheeks create a child-like look. The eyes are stabbed deep to add expression.

From the artist: Today is Octoberfest. The boy is dressed in his festival outfit and cannot wait to go. He tries to ride his rocking horse all the way there.

Russian Grandmother Holding Black Cat

Artist: Kawo@@

Artist Tip

I added embroidered flowers to the babushka to show the collaboration of wool felt and embroidery floss. Emphasize the cheek area to create this expressive smile. I added a lot of wool to the nose to create clear-cut features for this grandmother.

From the artist: A Russian grandmother wearing a babushka was the model for this doll. She is smiling as she looks at the black cat sleeping on her lap.

Spring Children

Artist: Usako Keno

Artist Tip

To make these flower-inspired fairy dresses, wet felt felket to make felt sheet. Cut petal shapes for the skirt and then stab each petal to the body overlapping the petal edges. Processed felket is also used to make the bodice of the dresses and to add flower petal hats as well.

From the artist: These girls are wearing petal-like dresses, which are made with spring in mind. The ability to create shapes and mix colors are advantages of using felt.

Loretta Lost in a World of Dreams

Artist: mille

Artist Tip

I like to use simple techniques to emphasize cute features in my dolls. A sweet rabbit hat made from processed wool felket, braided hair, and a big felket bow add to the whimsical charm of this doll.

From the artist: In Loretta's dreamworld, she plays with all manner of imaginary creatures.

About the Author
Mihoko Ueno

Known for her whimsical characters and lifelike animals, Mihoko's goal is to make dolls that will bring joy to those who hold them. She is currently experimenting with bringing her dolls to life with stop-motion animation. She sells her work throughout shops in Tokyo.